SUSAN RESSLER

EXECUTIVE ORDER

Images of 1970s Corporate America

with an essay by Mark Rice

Daylight

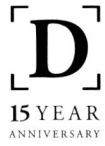

D
15 YEAR
ANNIVERSARY

Cofounders: Taj Forer and Michael Itkoff
Creative director: Ursula Damm
Copy editors: Nancy Hubbard, Barbara Richard

Photographs © Susan Ressler, 1977–1980

These images first preceded and were then part of a 1979–80 National Endowment for the Arts sponsored survey intended to document Los Angeles during its Bicentennial, including the artist's portrayal of what is now recognized as an epochal and historically important period in the growth of corporate America. The subjects depicted herein generously provided their consent to be photographed in order to participate in the original project, and the artist wishes to thank them for their indispensable support and cooperation.

"Executive Disorder" © Mark Rice, 2017

Printed by OFSET YAPIMEVI, Istanbul

Daylight Books
E-mail: info@daylightbooks.org
Web: www.daylightbooks.org

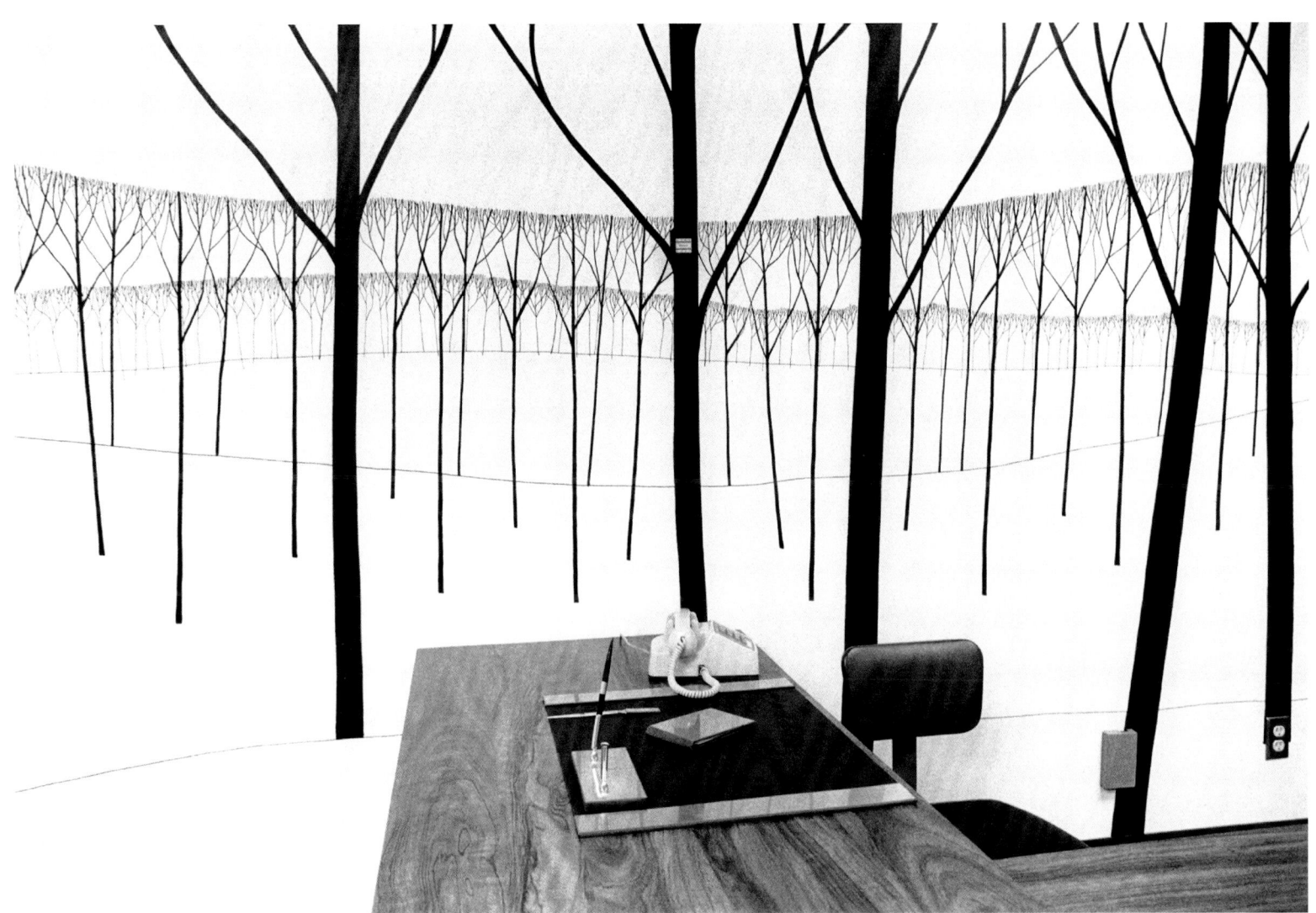

In 1977 I entered a bank to make a transaction

What I withdrew was a photograph

Columbia Savings and Loan

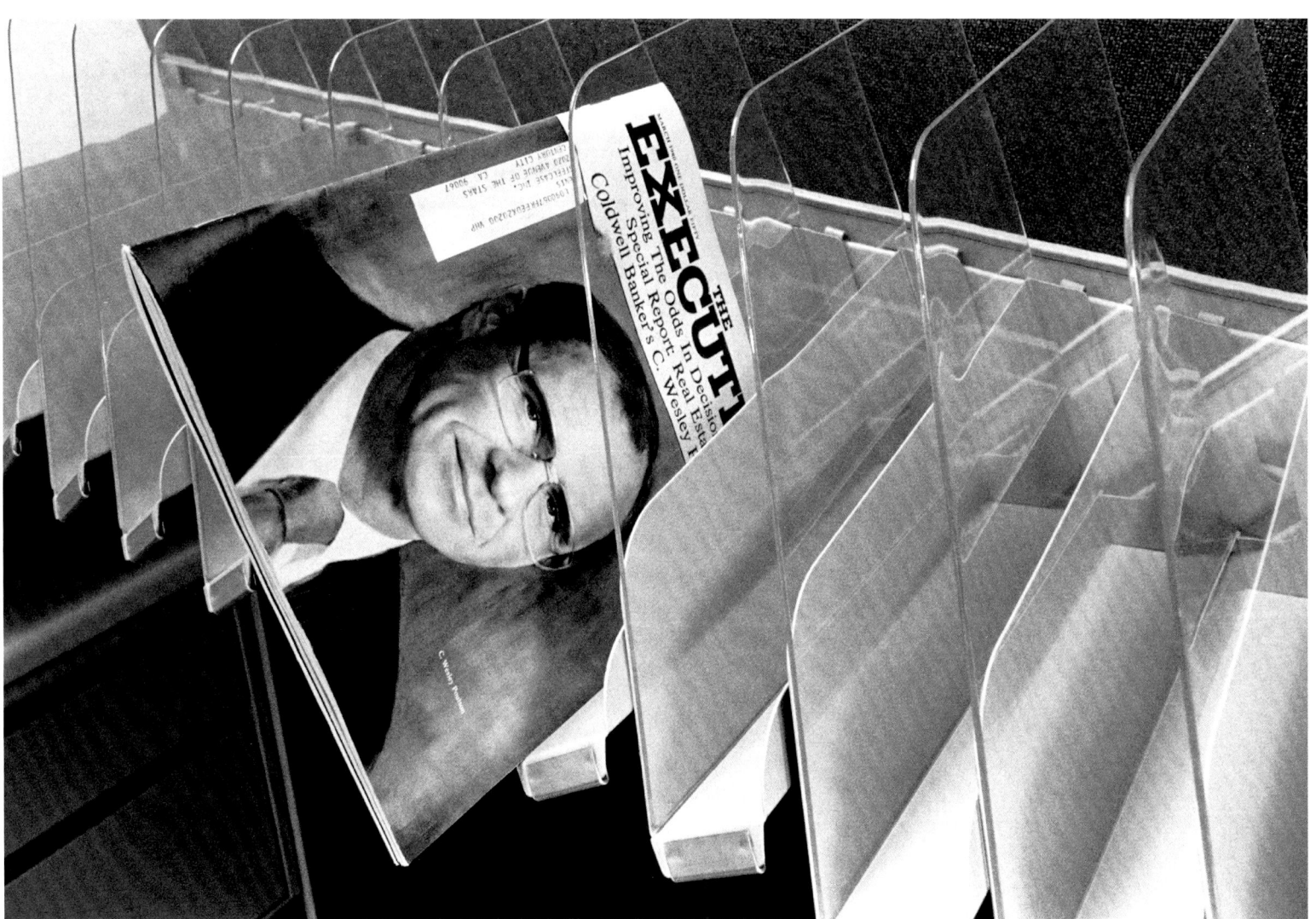

The Executive

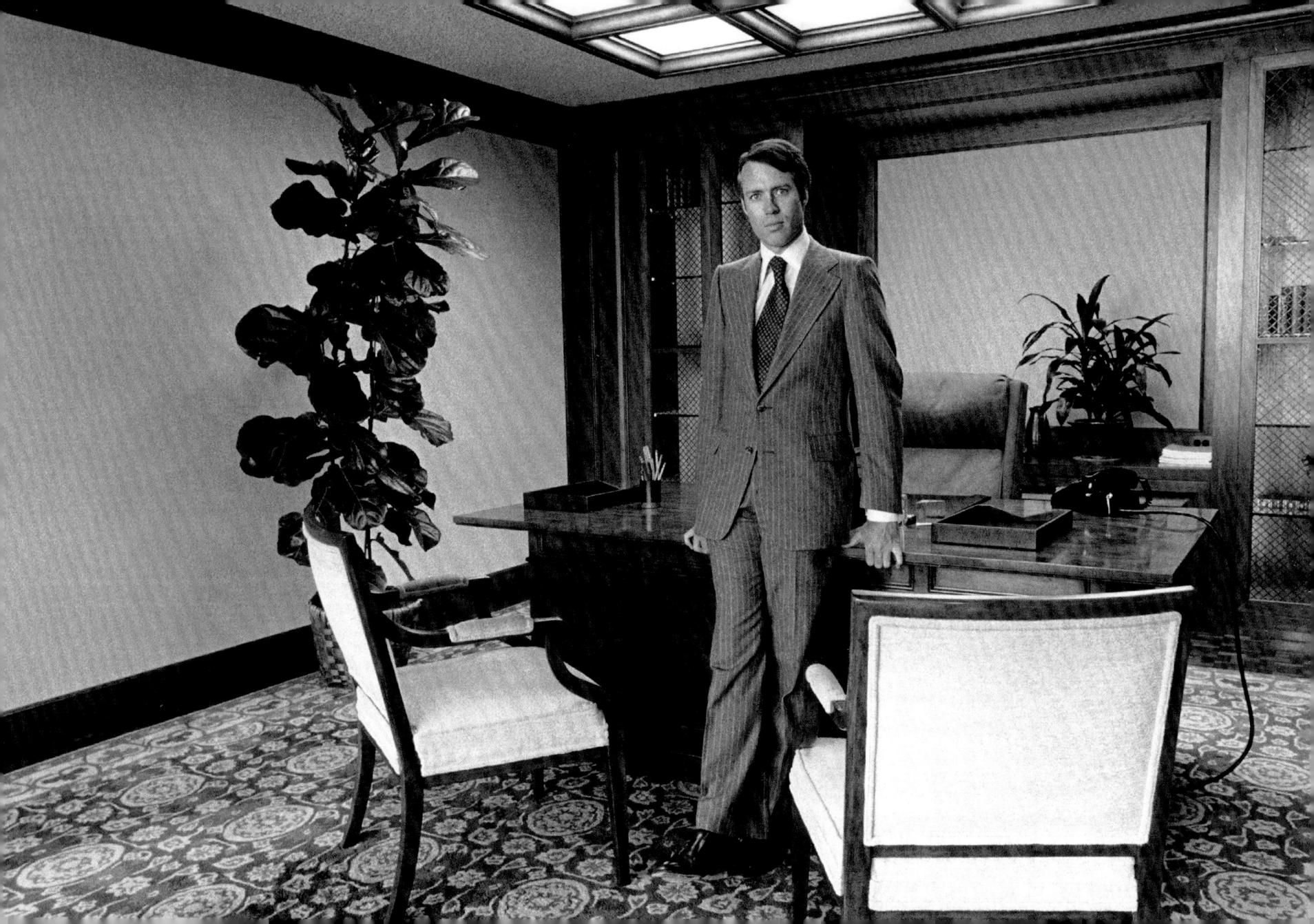

Jet Propelled

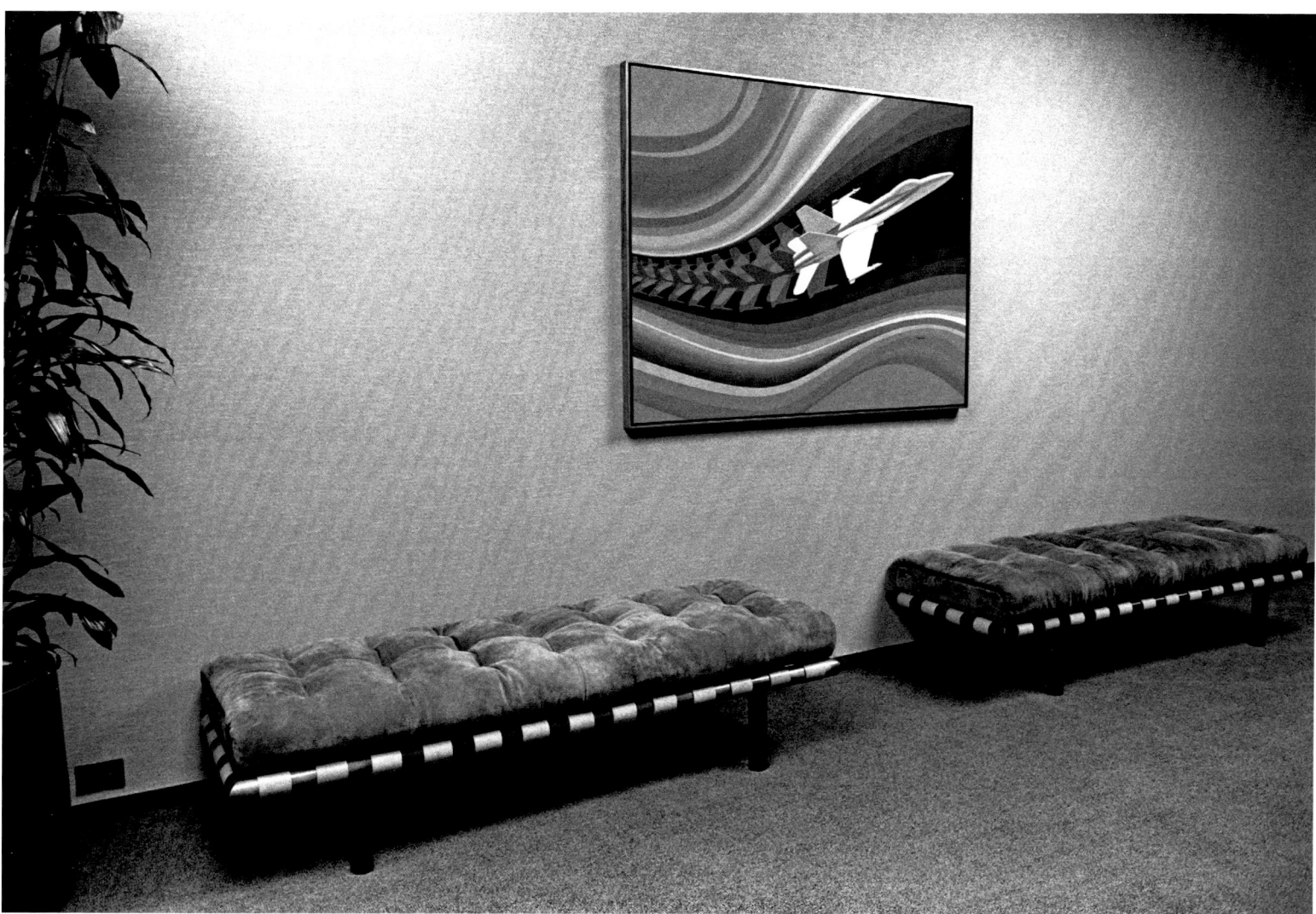

Wednesday

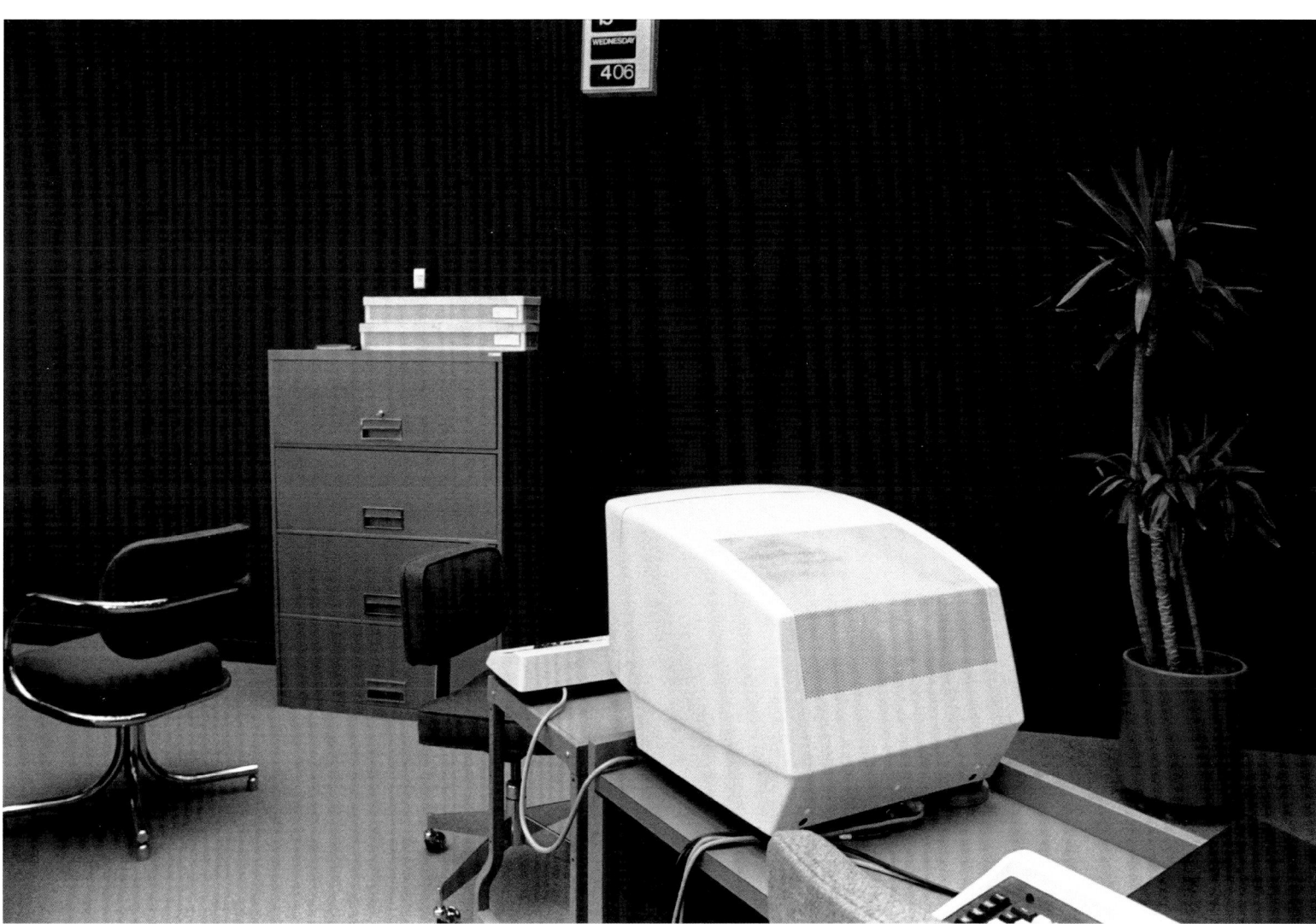

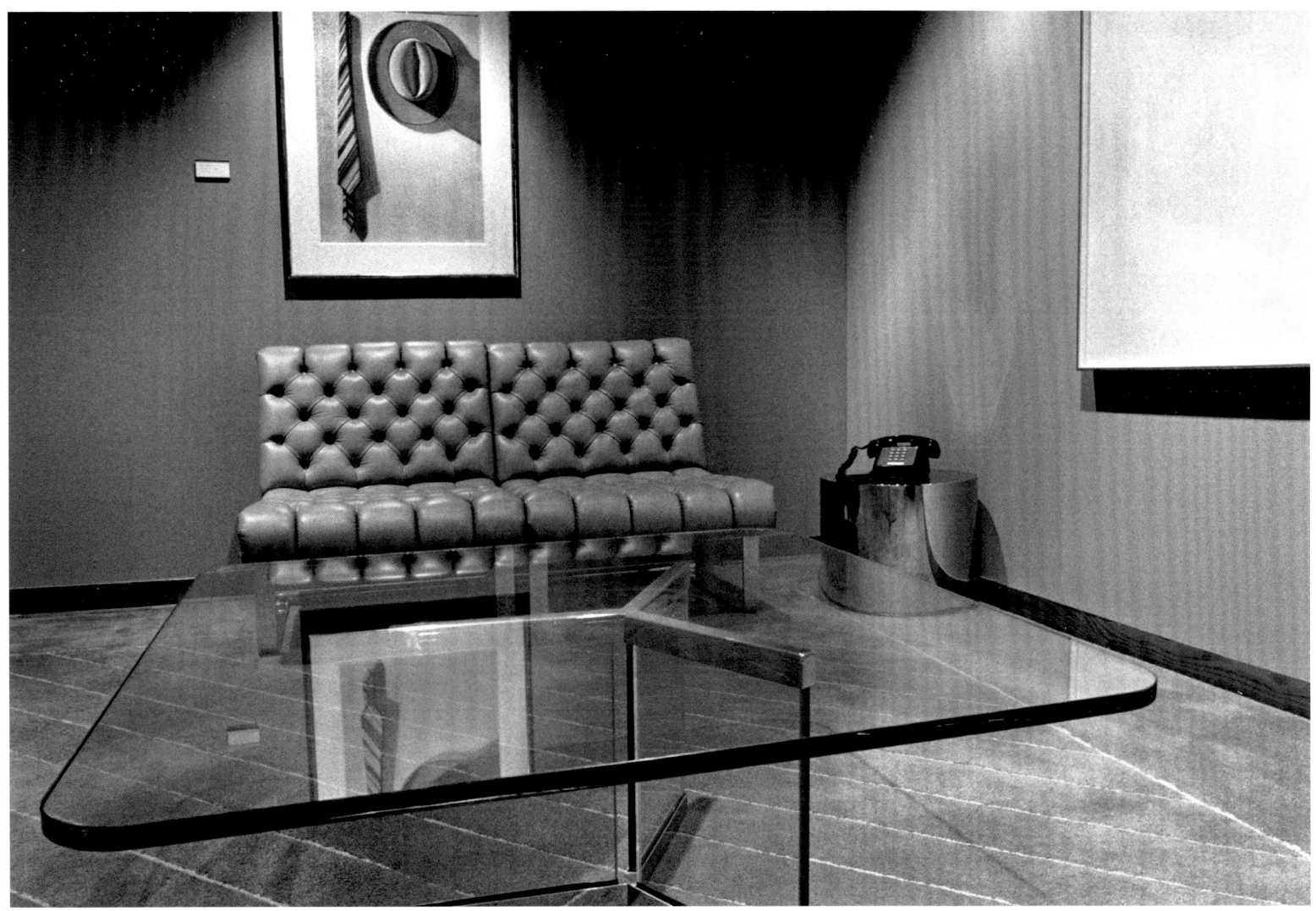

Hat and Tie

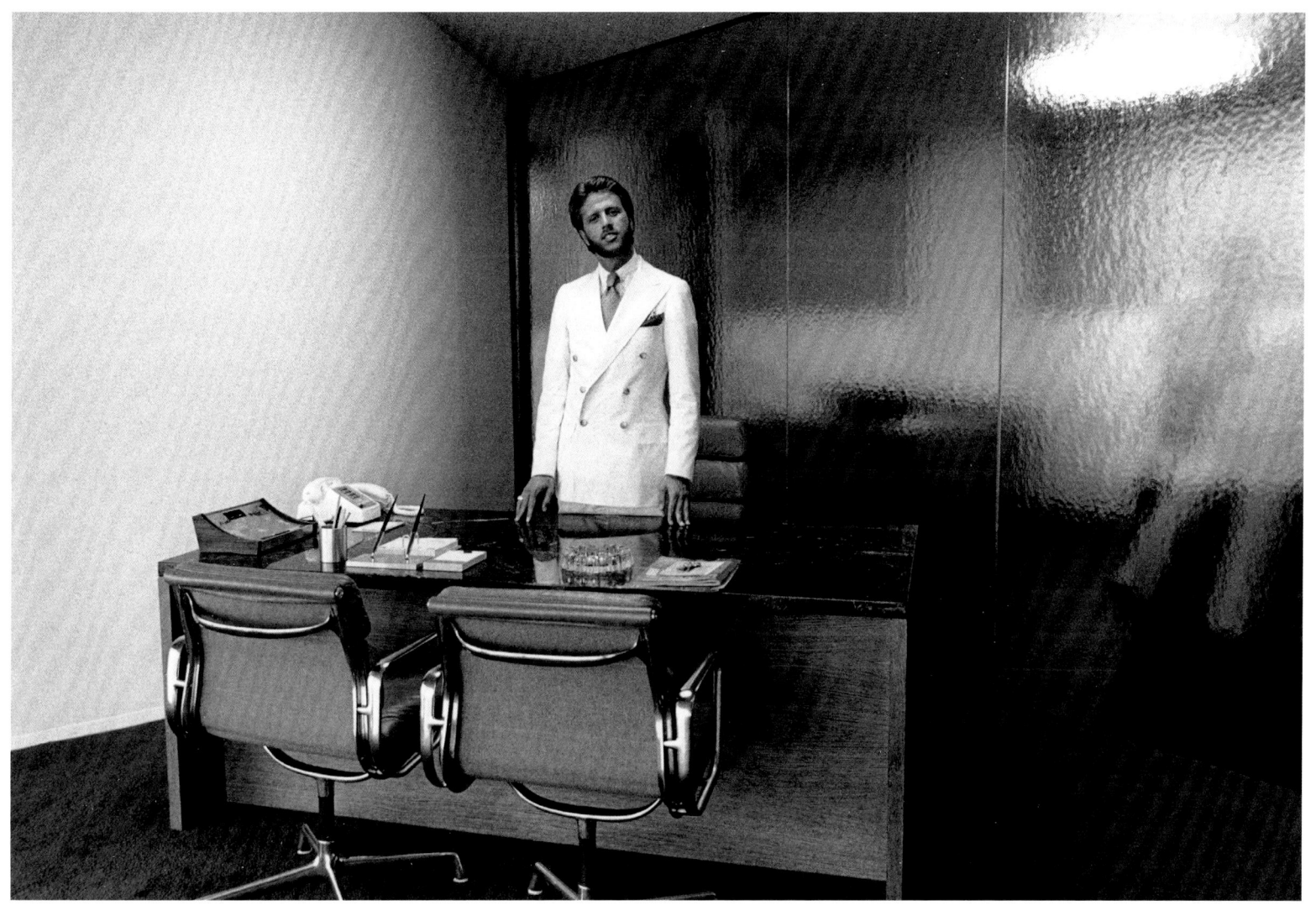

White Blazer

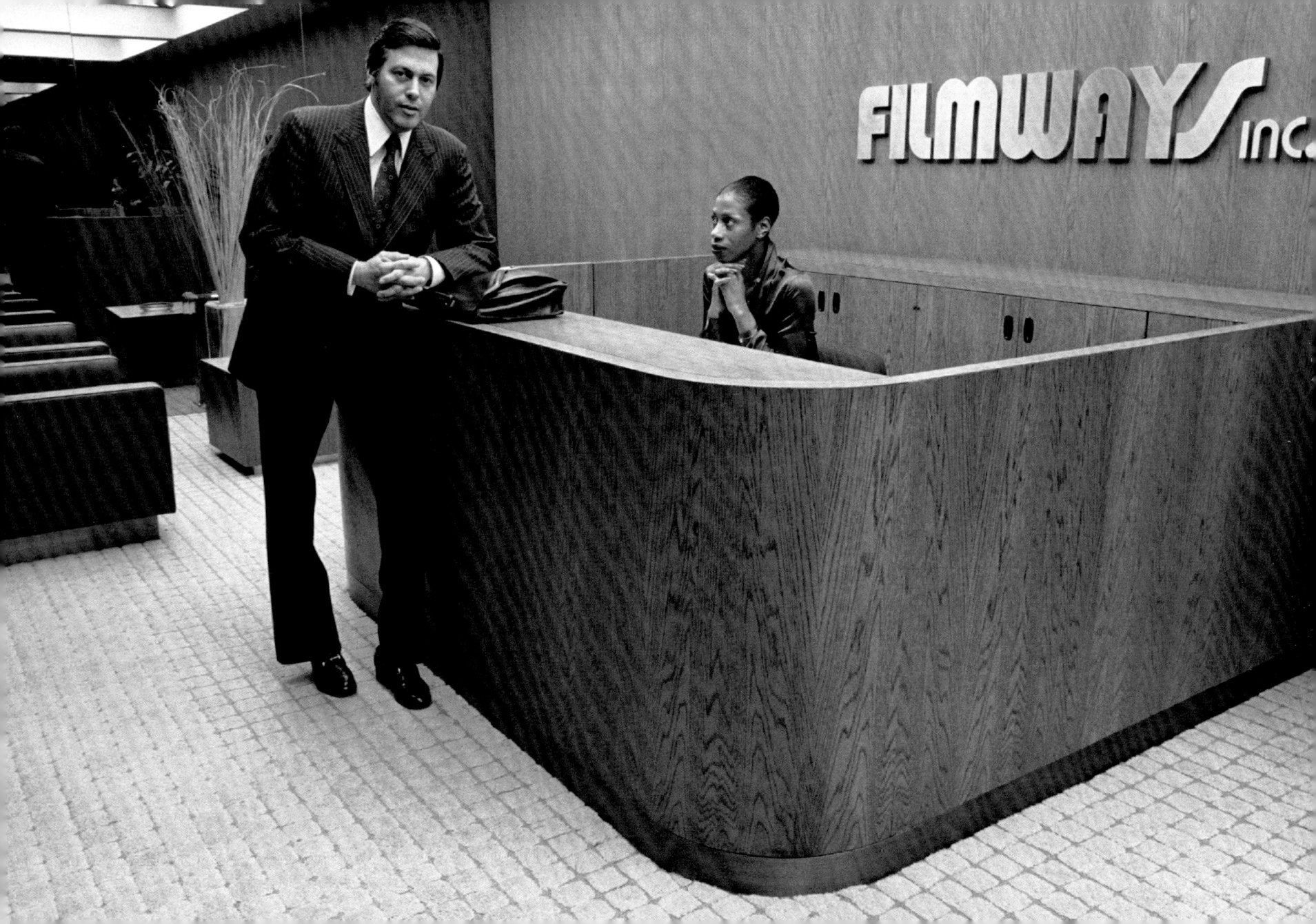

Reception

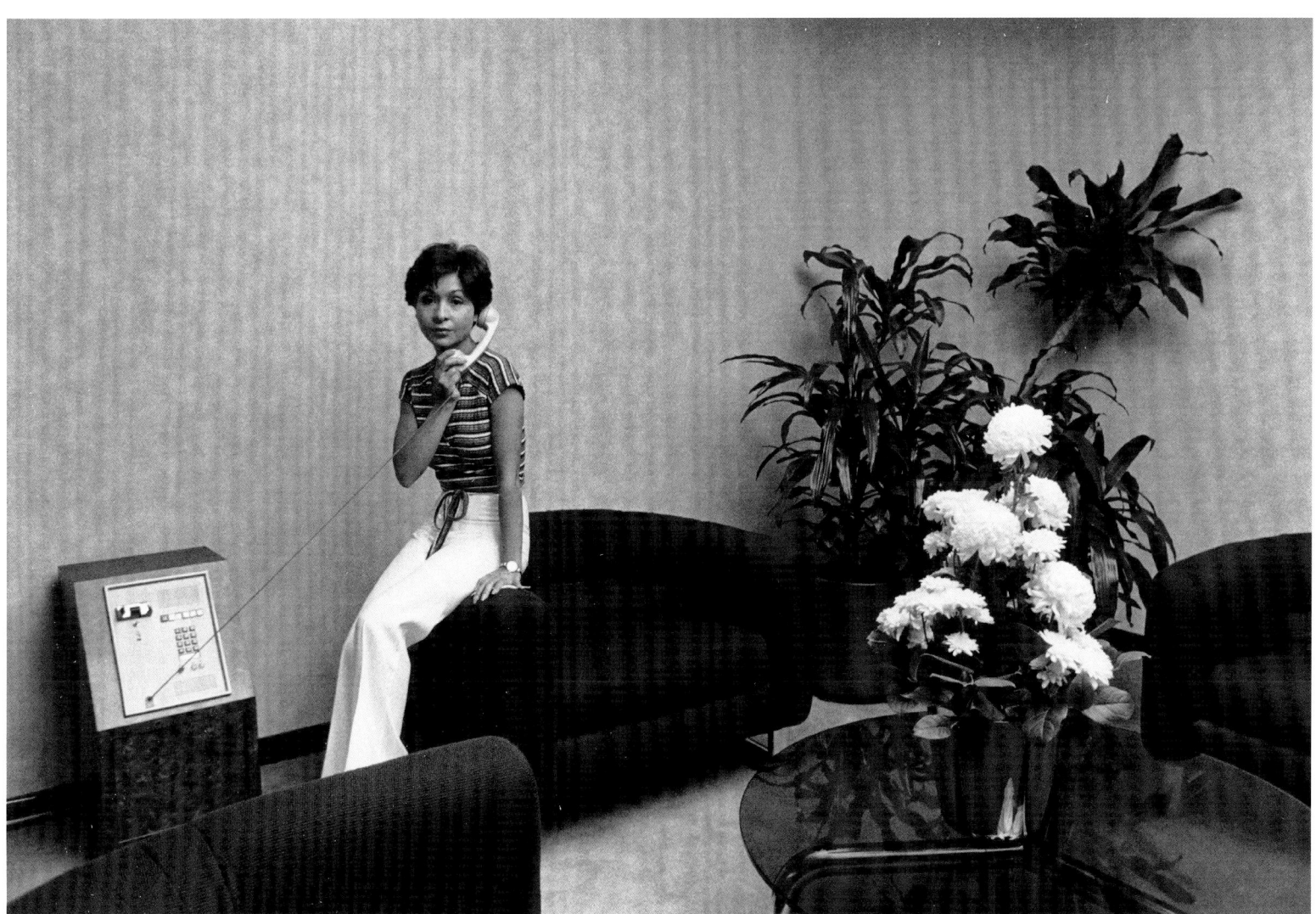

Languid Blonde

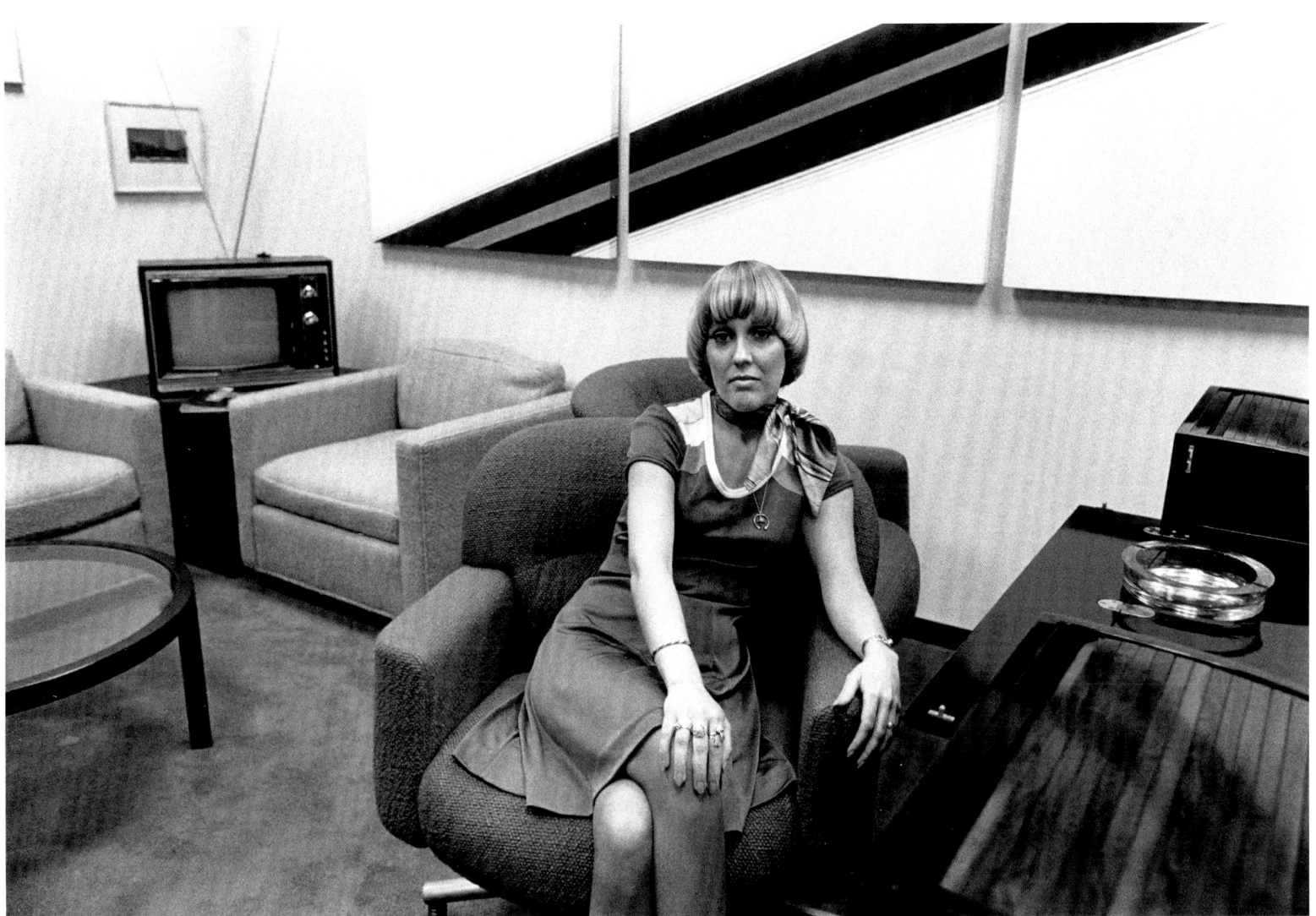

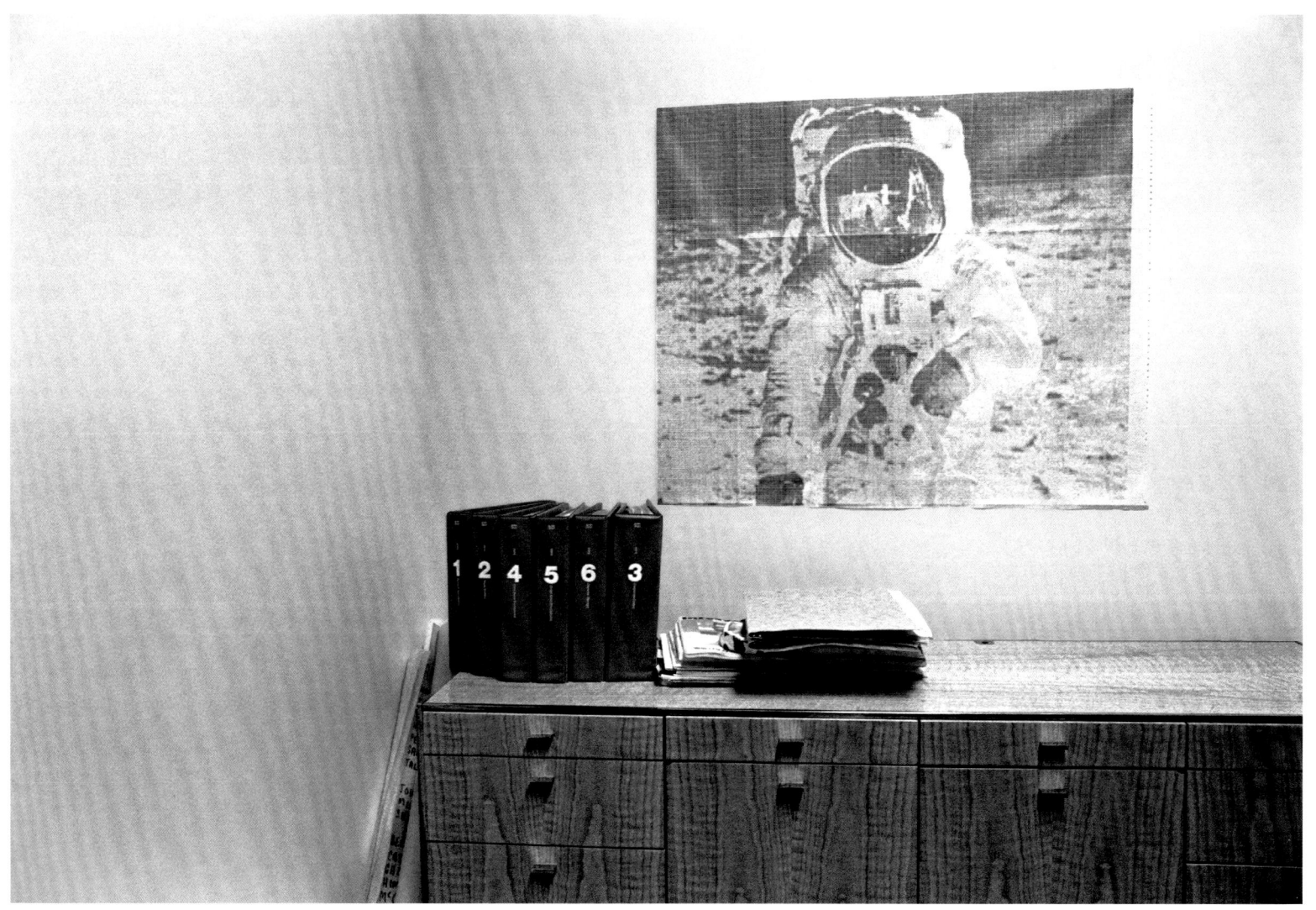

Countdown

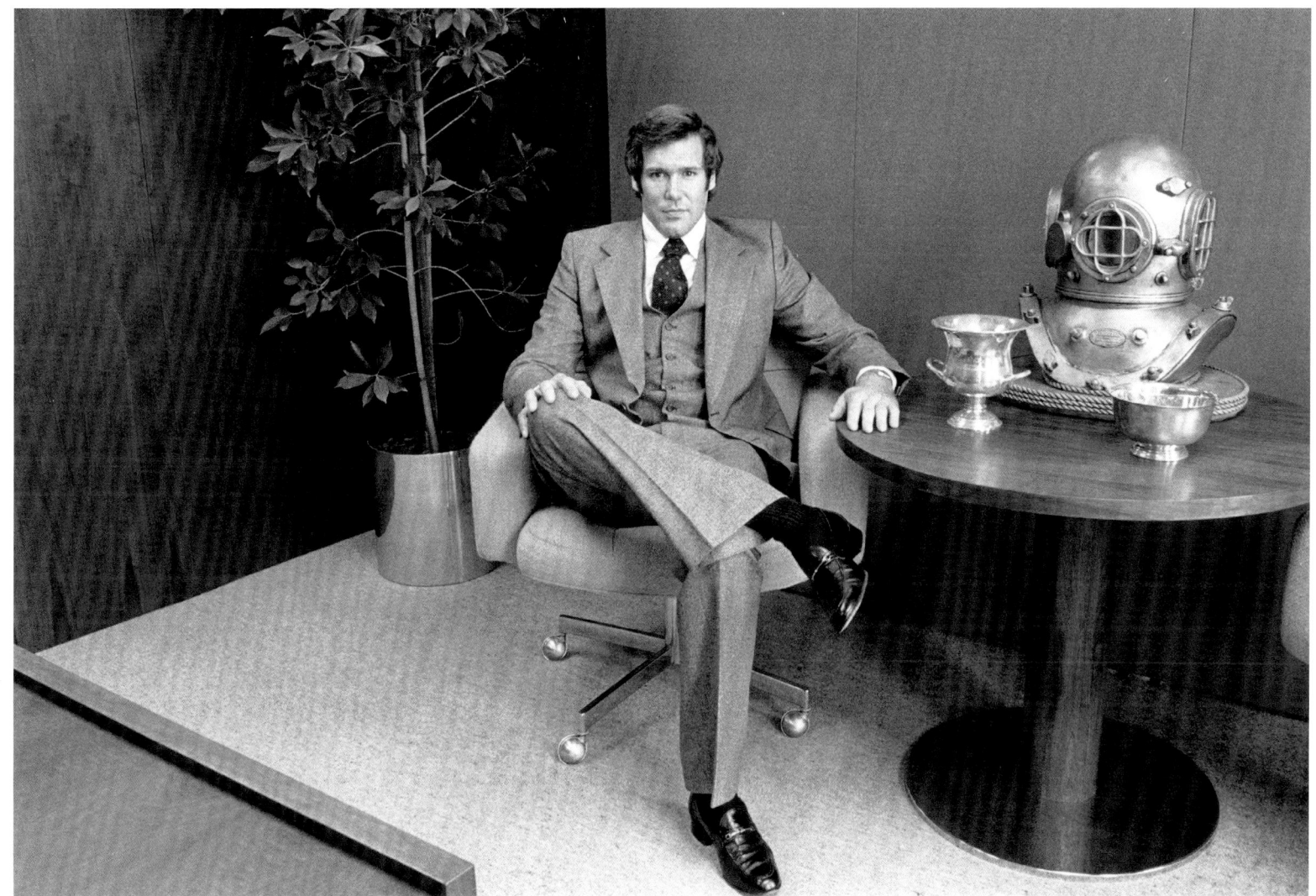

Diver

Podium

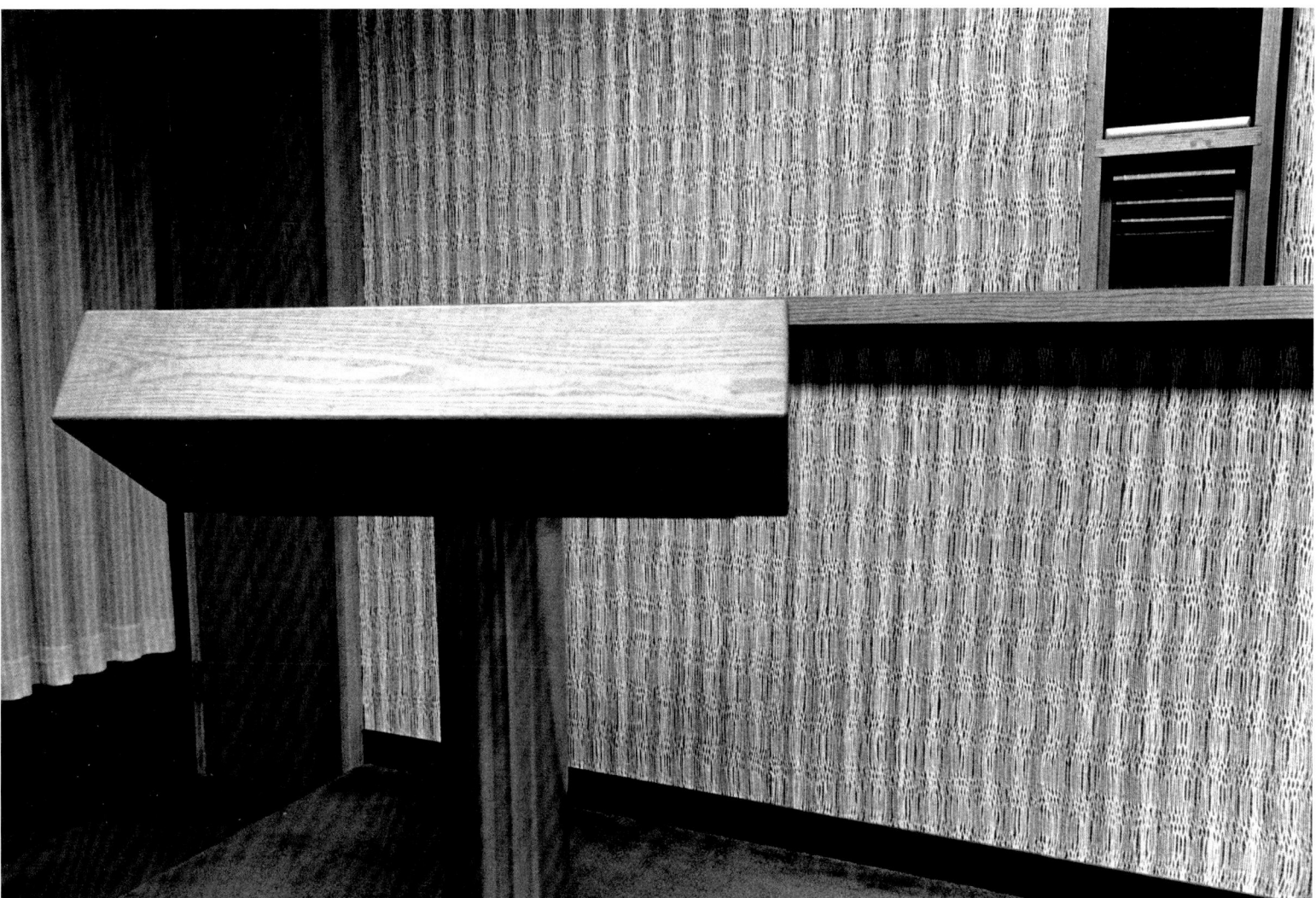

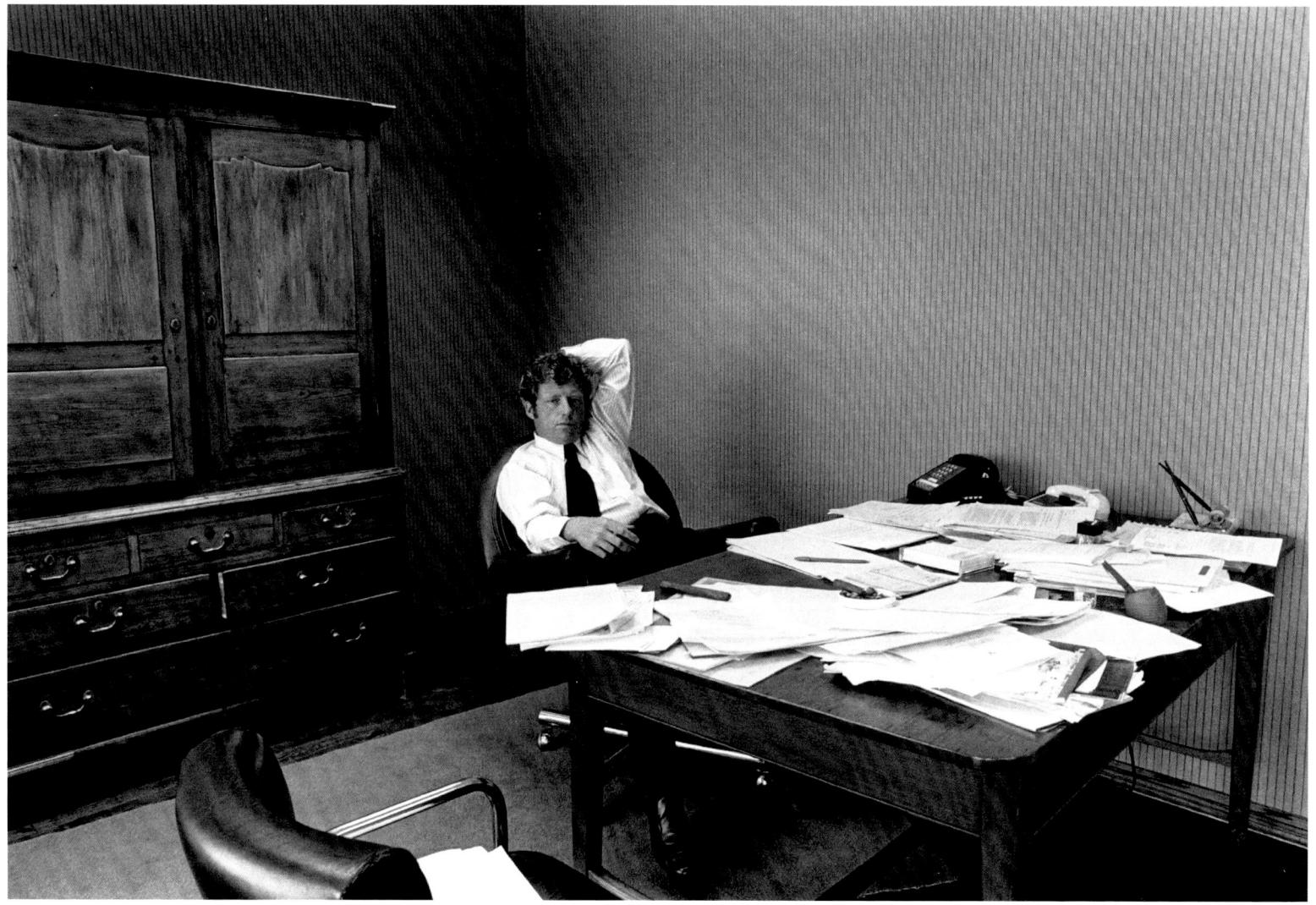

Lawyer

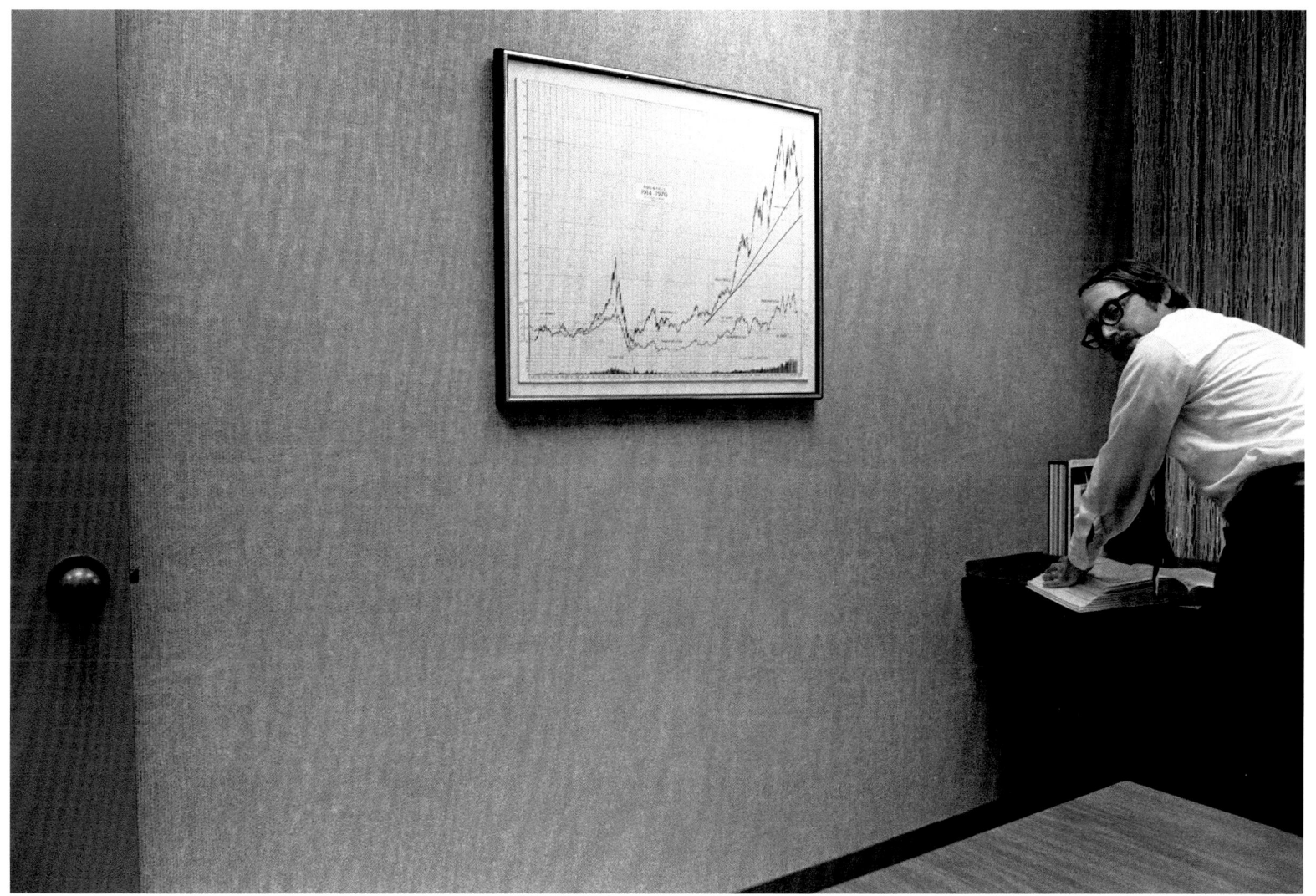

Graphing Gains

Ornament

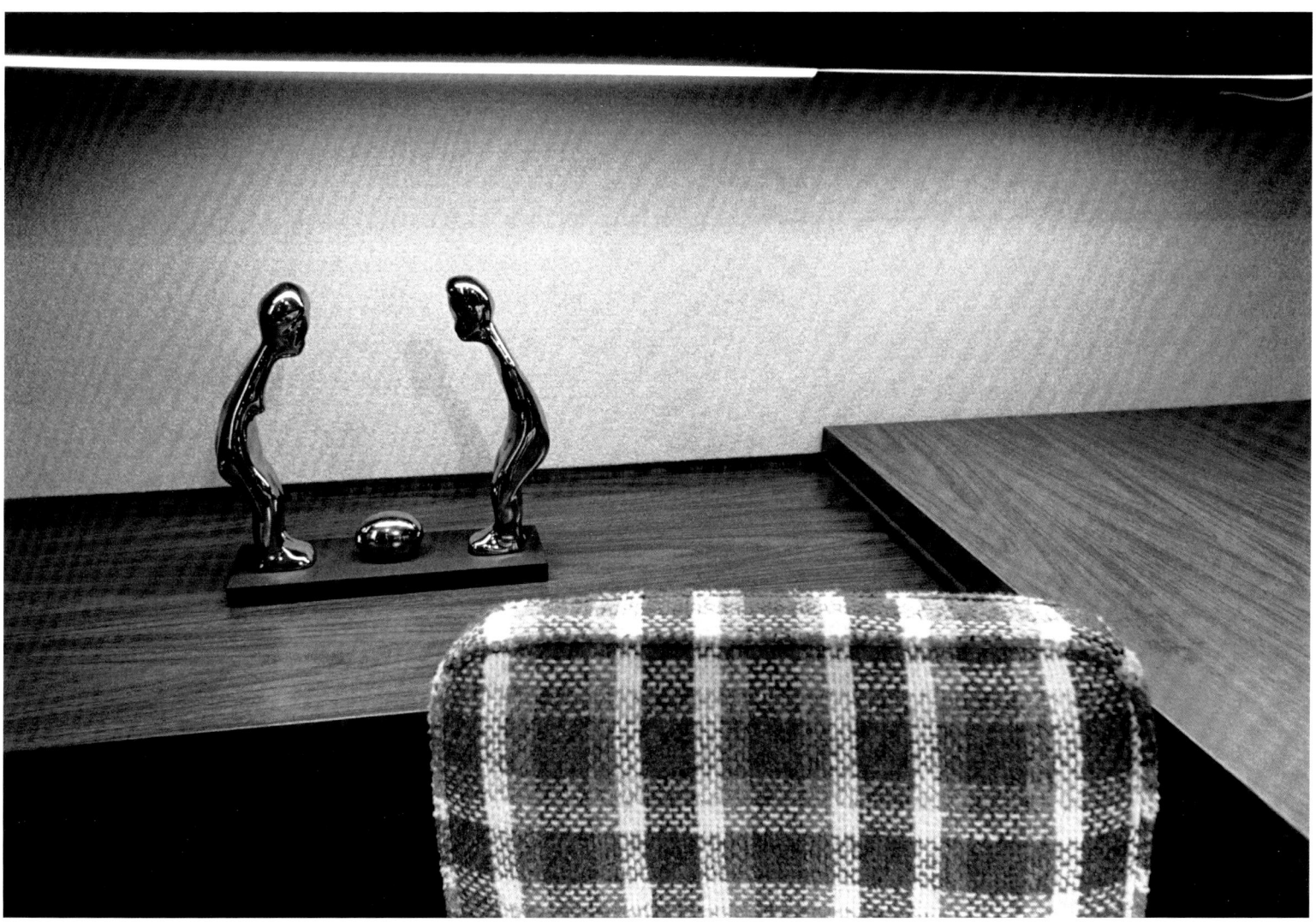

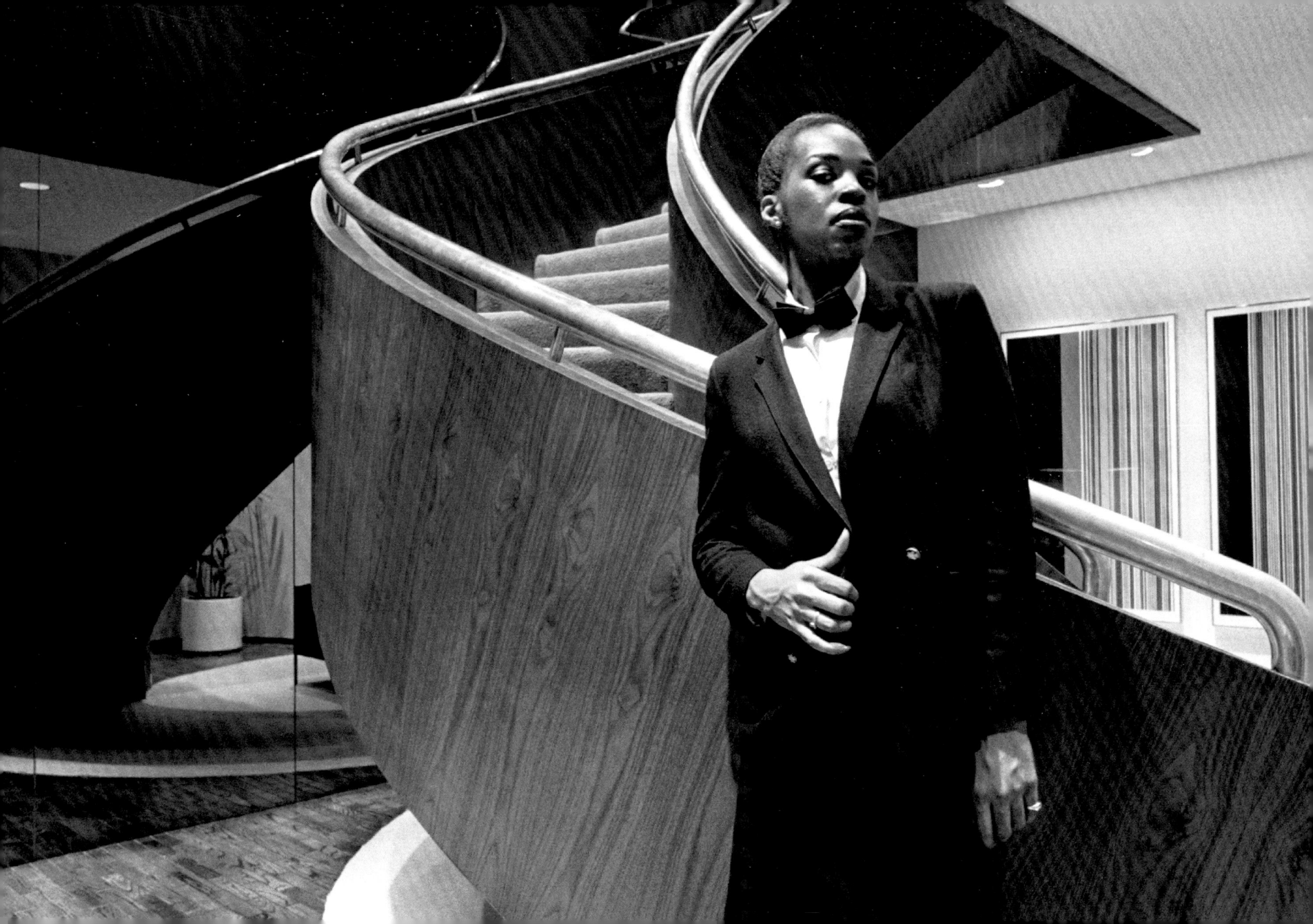

Bow Tie

Zen

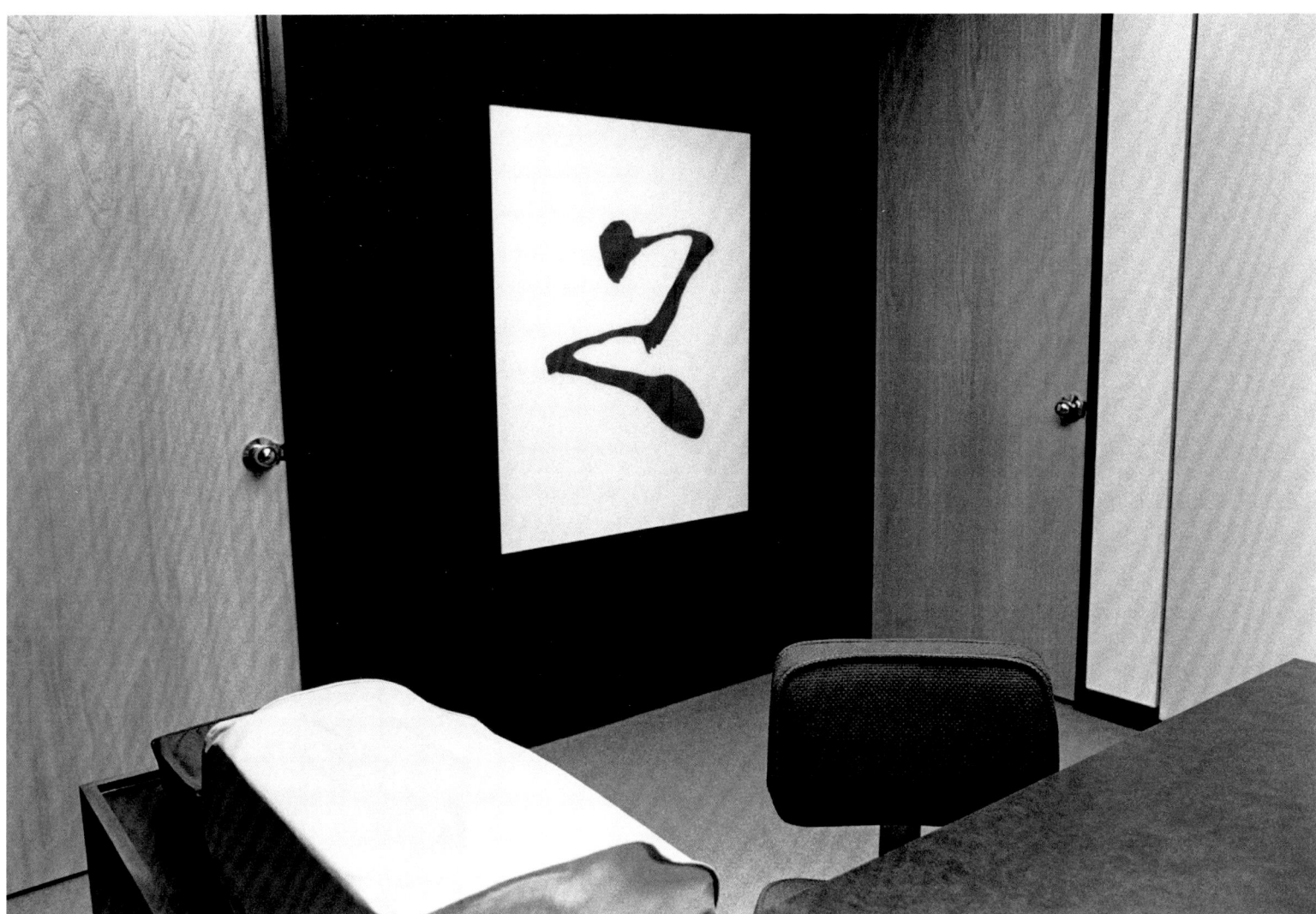

The Capital Group
(from the Los Angeles Documentary Project)

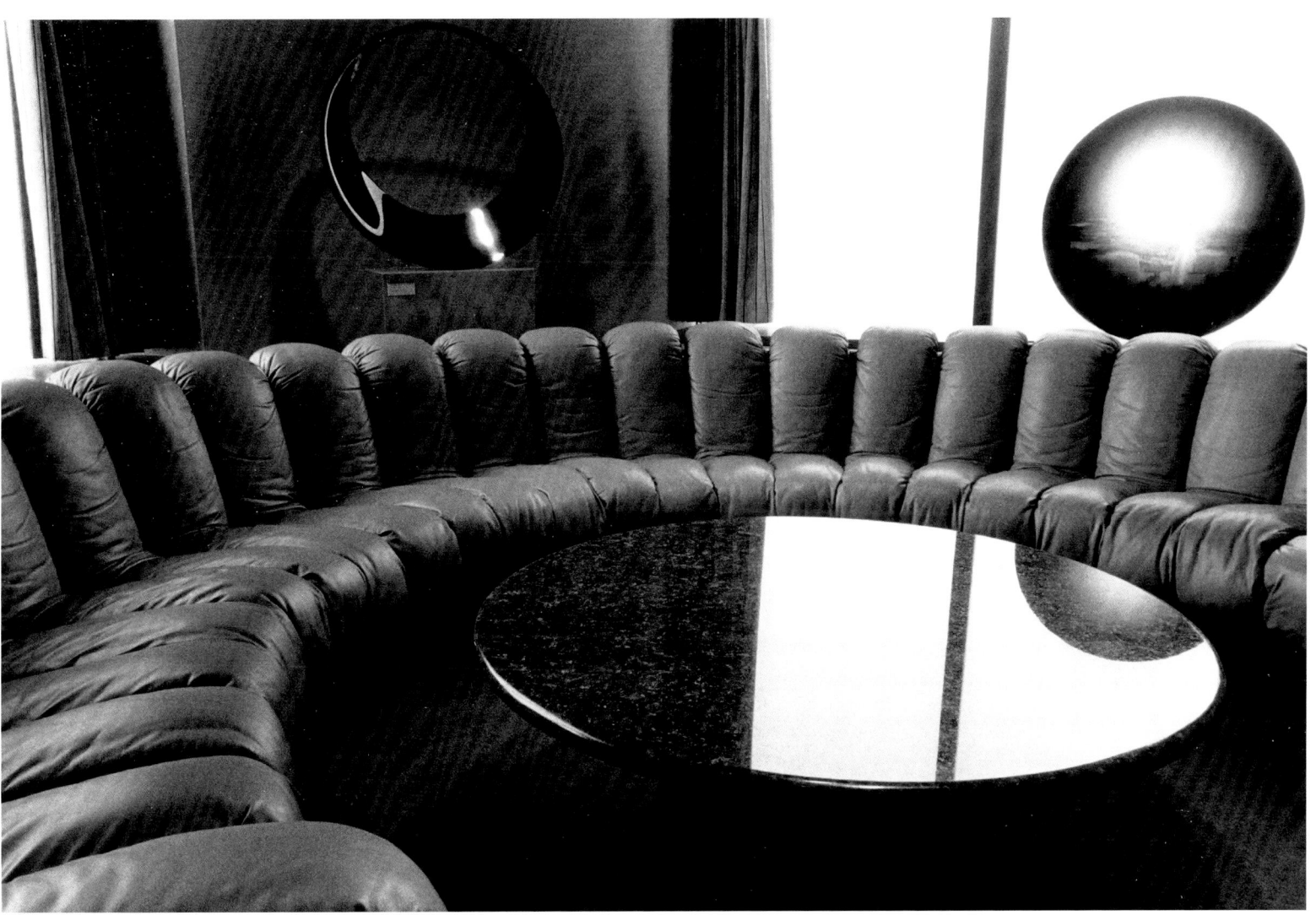

Steelcase
(from the Los Angeles Documentary Project)

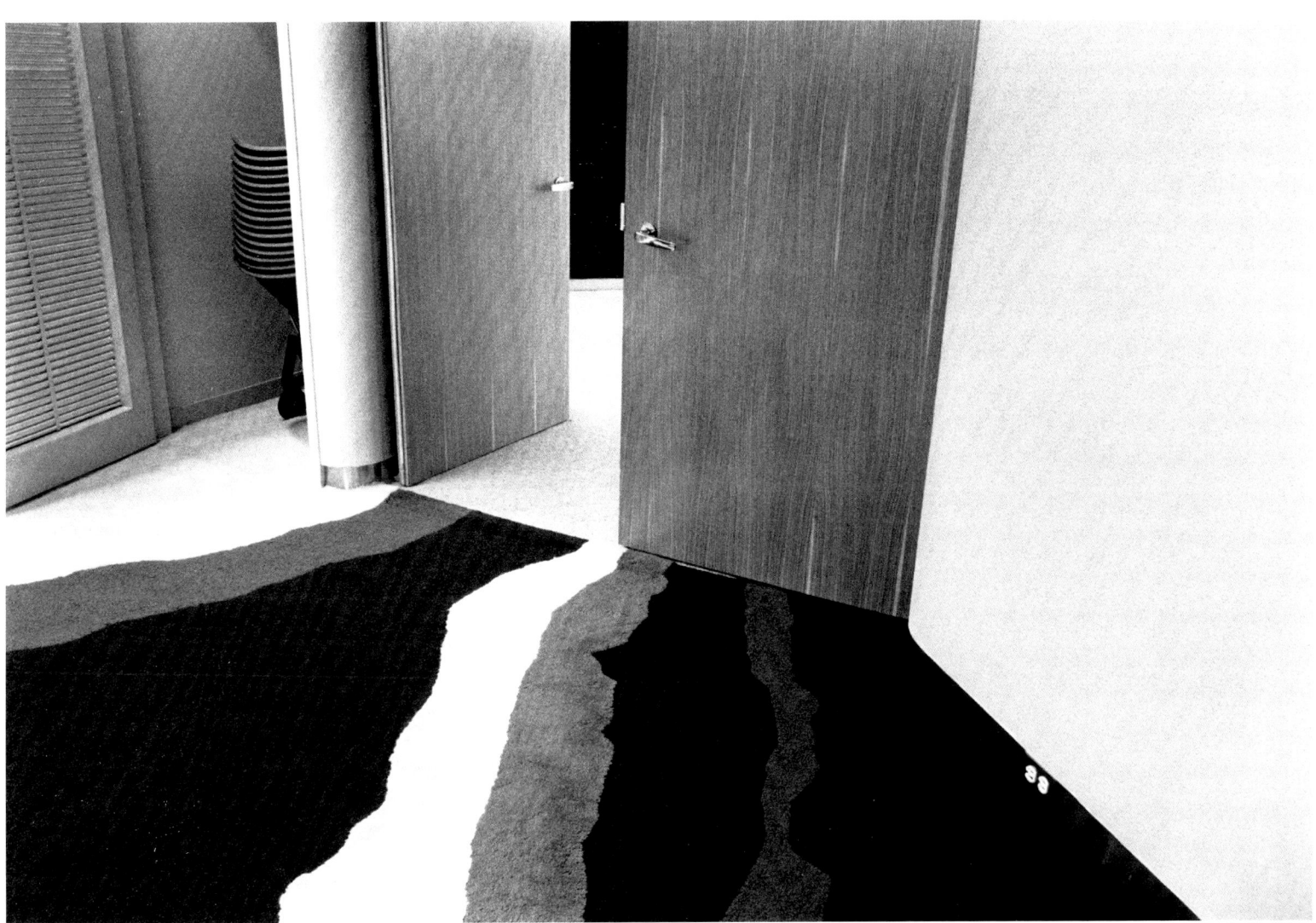

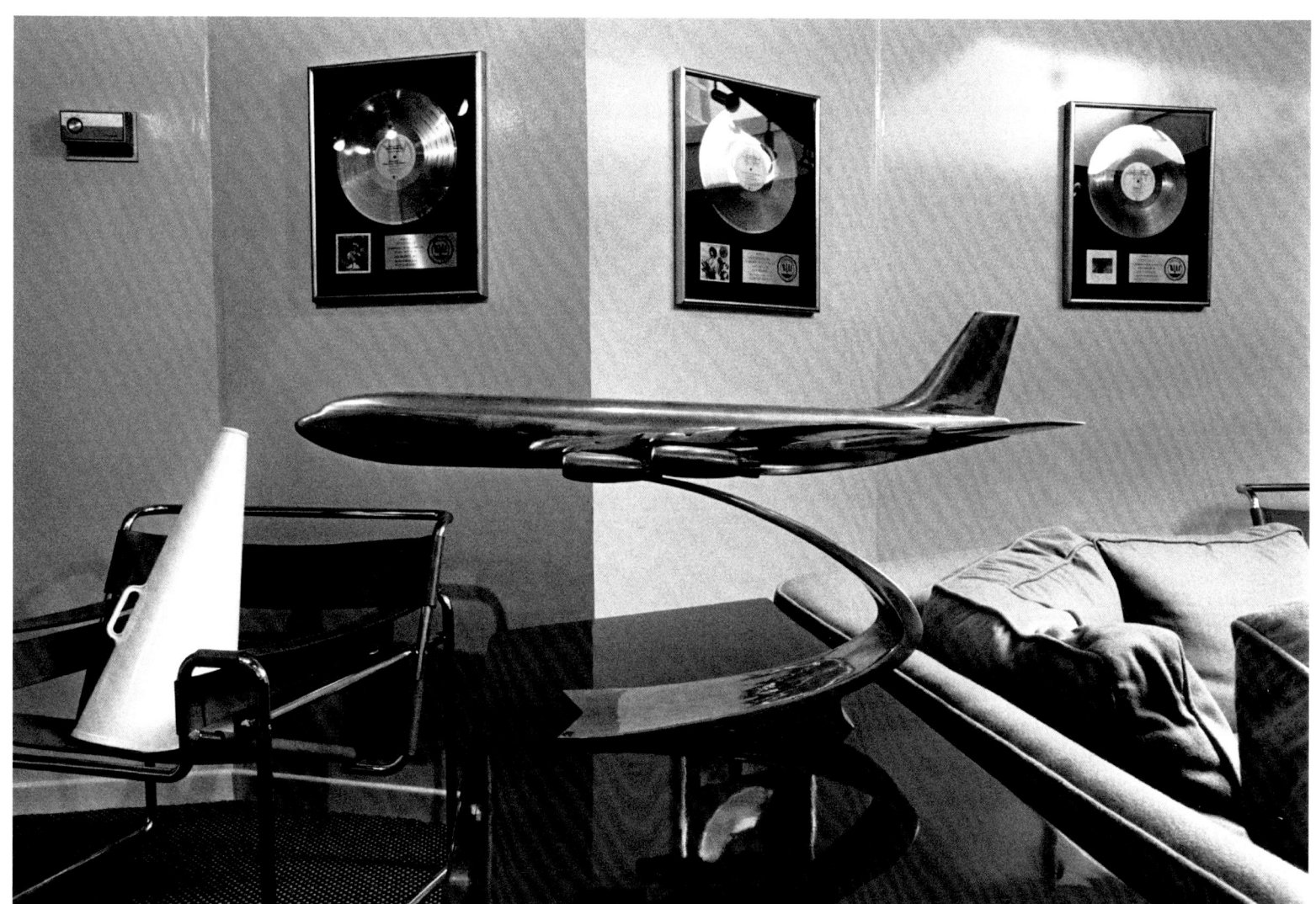

A&M Records
(from the Los Angeles Documentary Project)

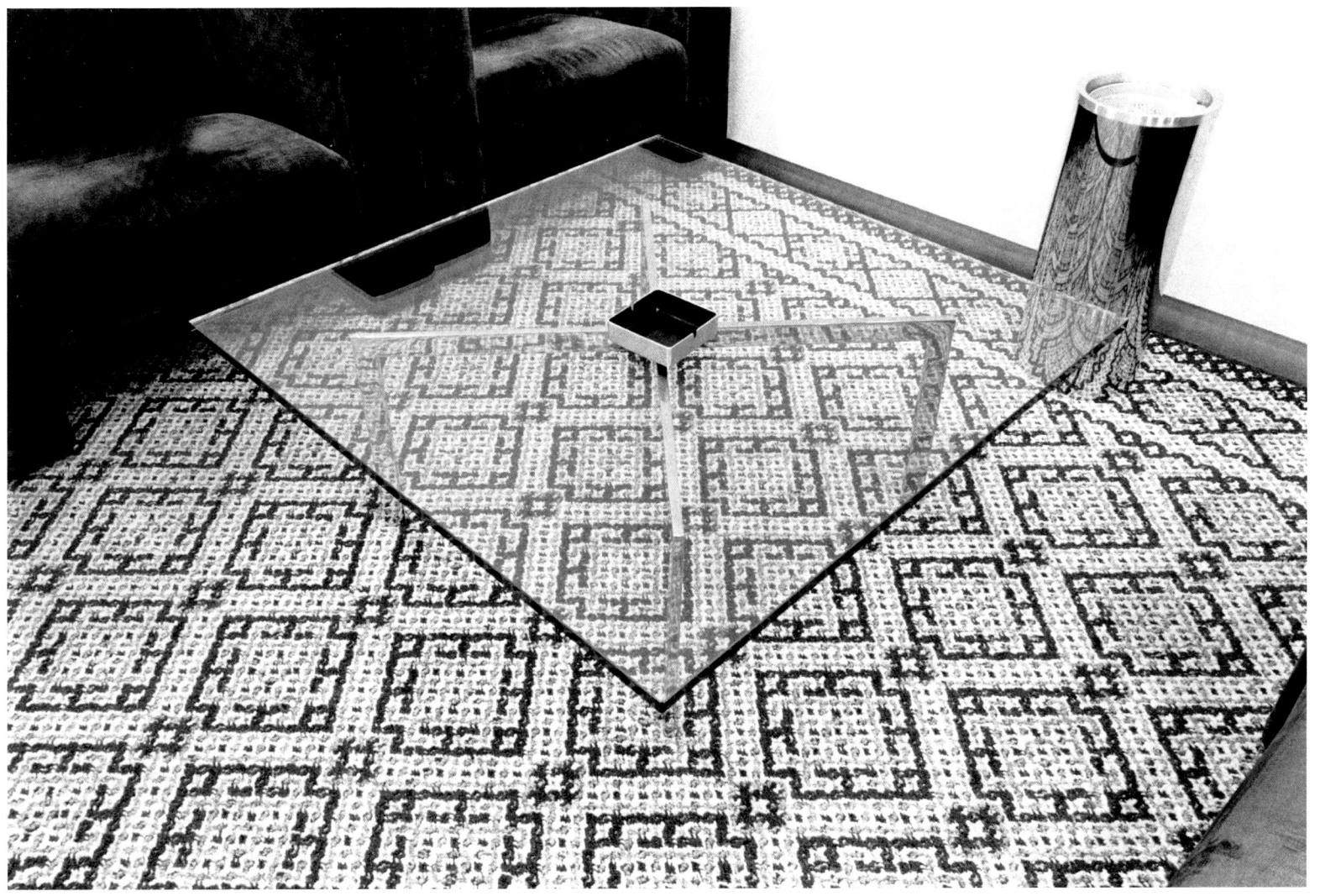

Kyowa Bank
(from the Los Angeles Documentary Project)

Vidal Sassoon
(from the Los Angeles Documentary Project)

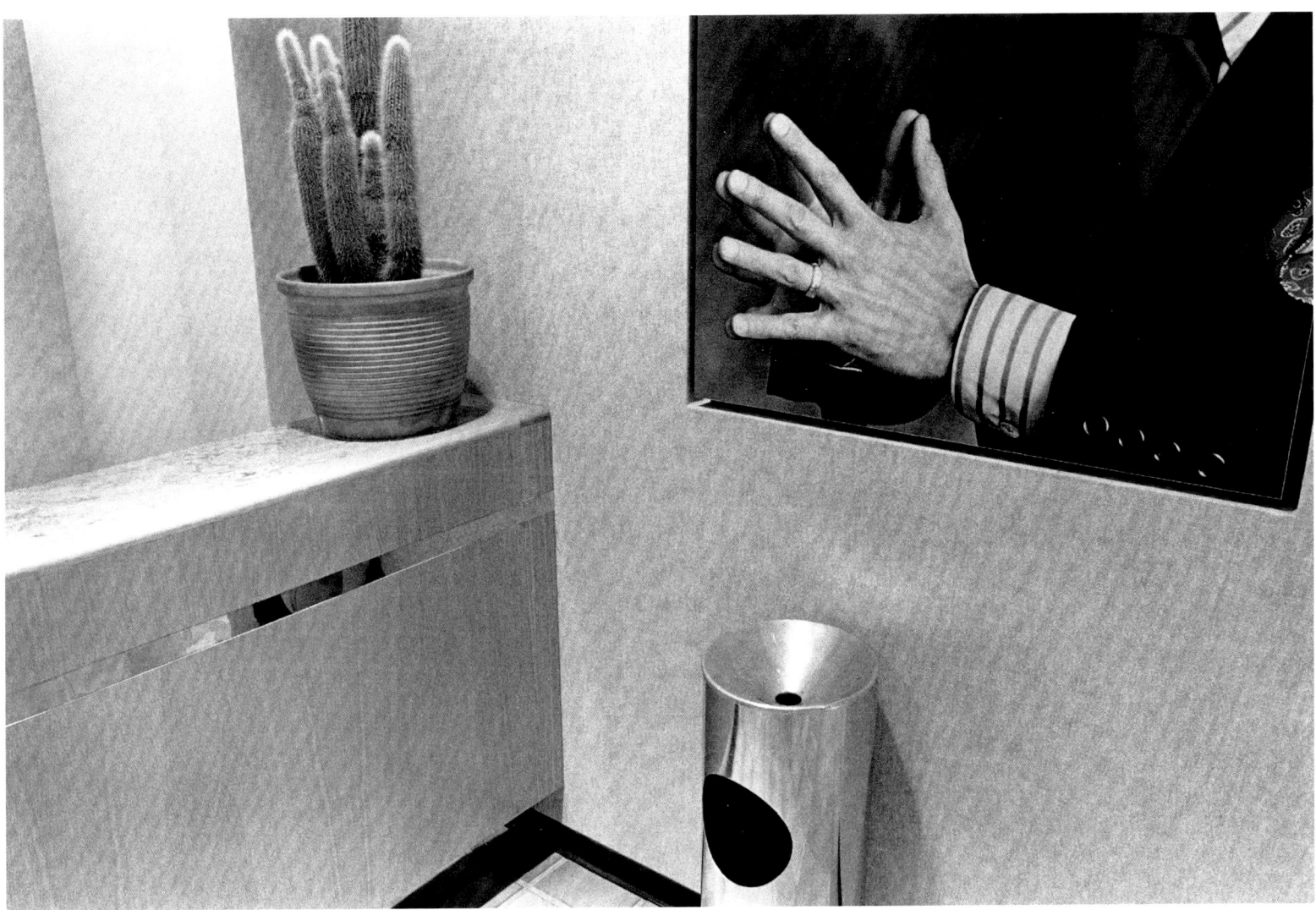

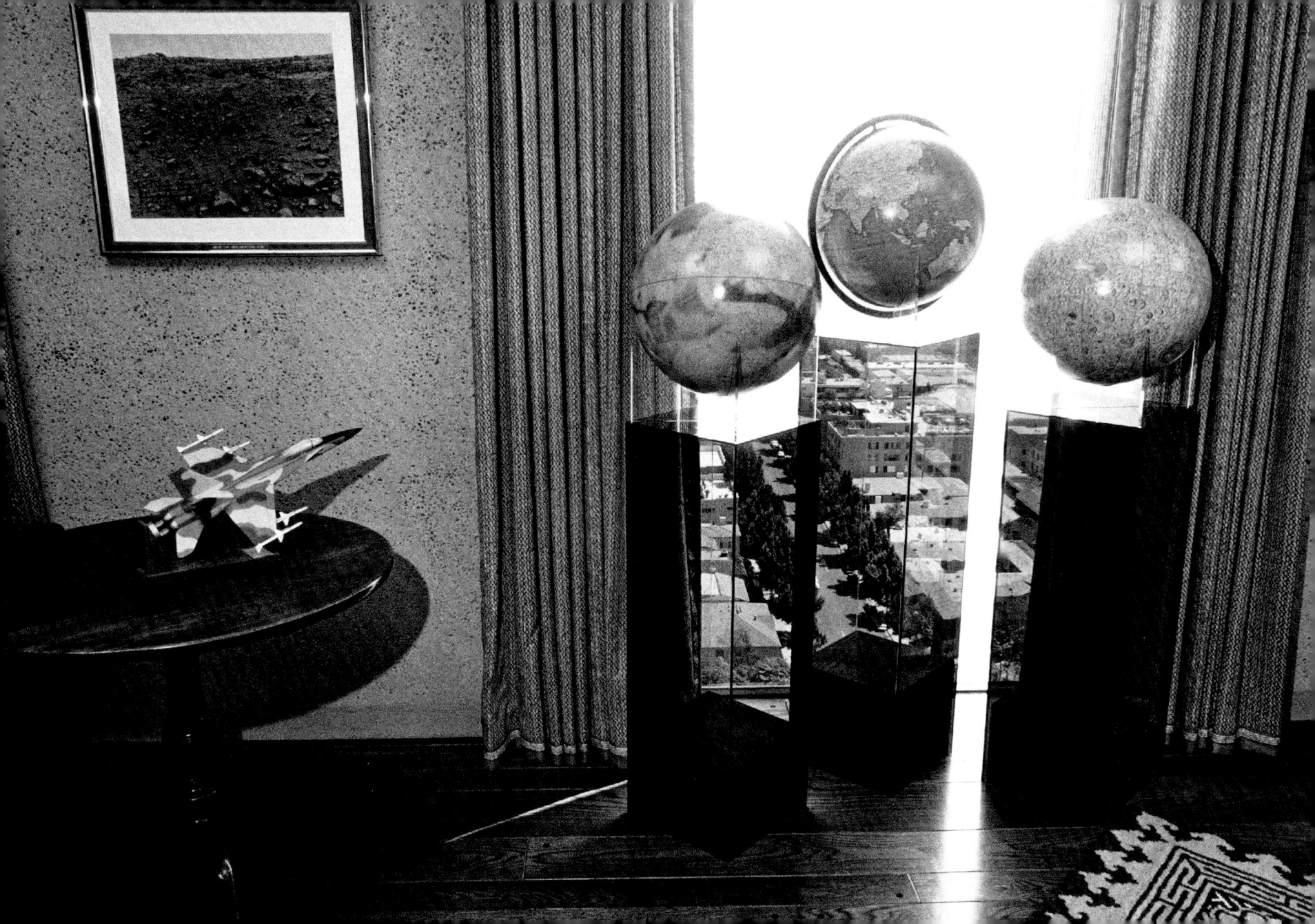

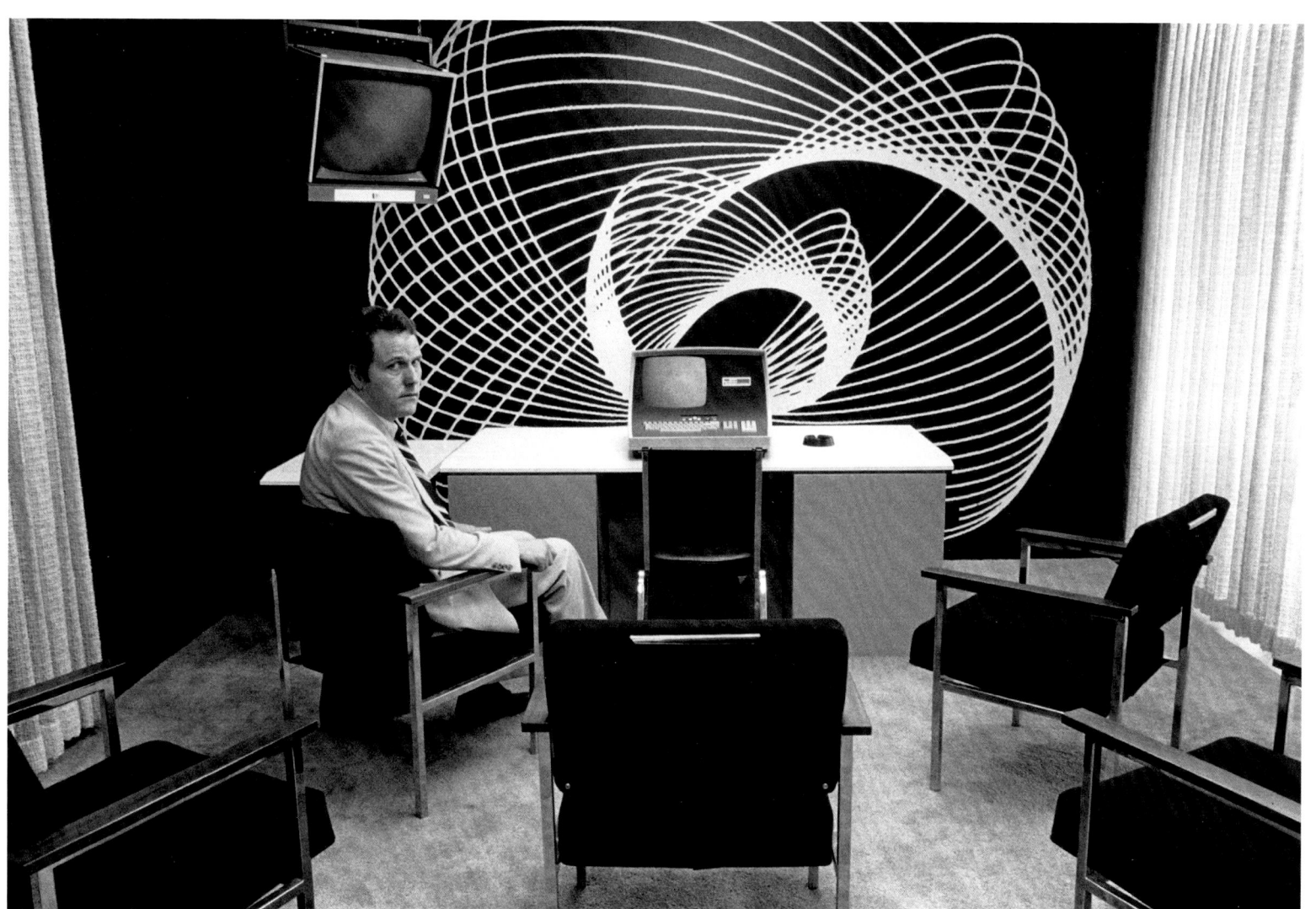

TRW
(from the Los Angeles Documentary Project)

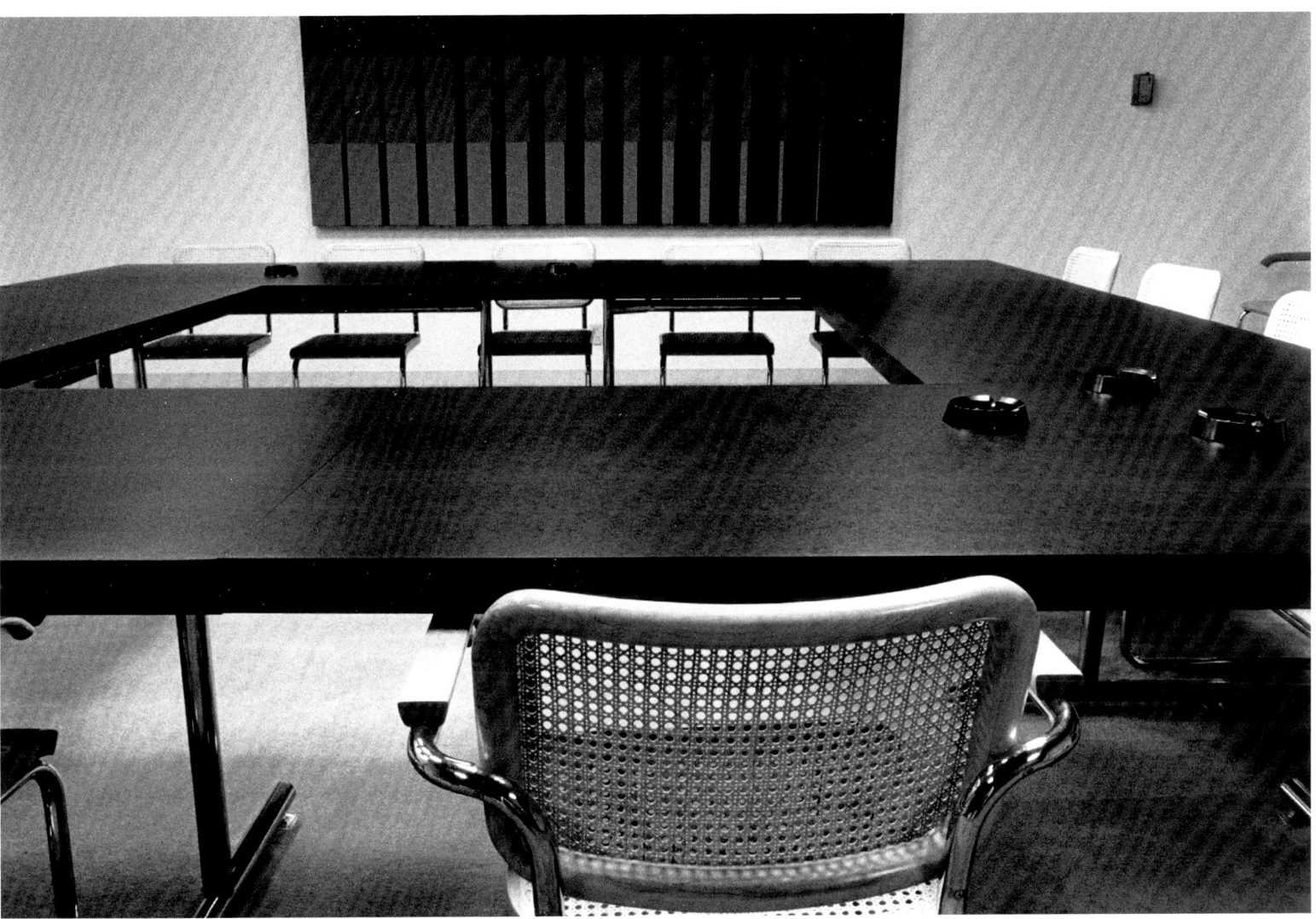

Honeywell
(from the Los Angeles Documentary Project)

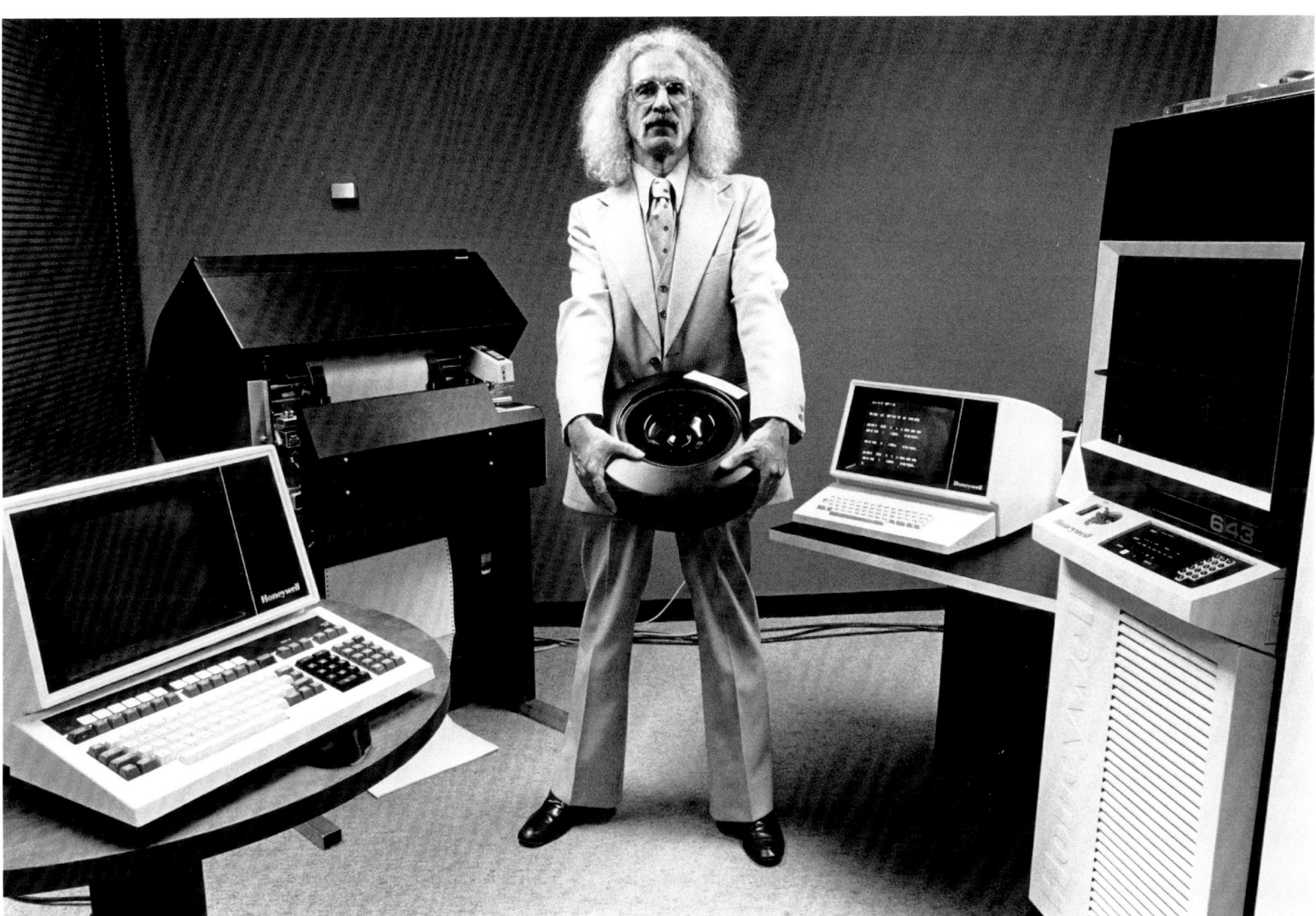

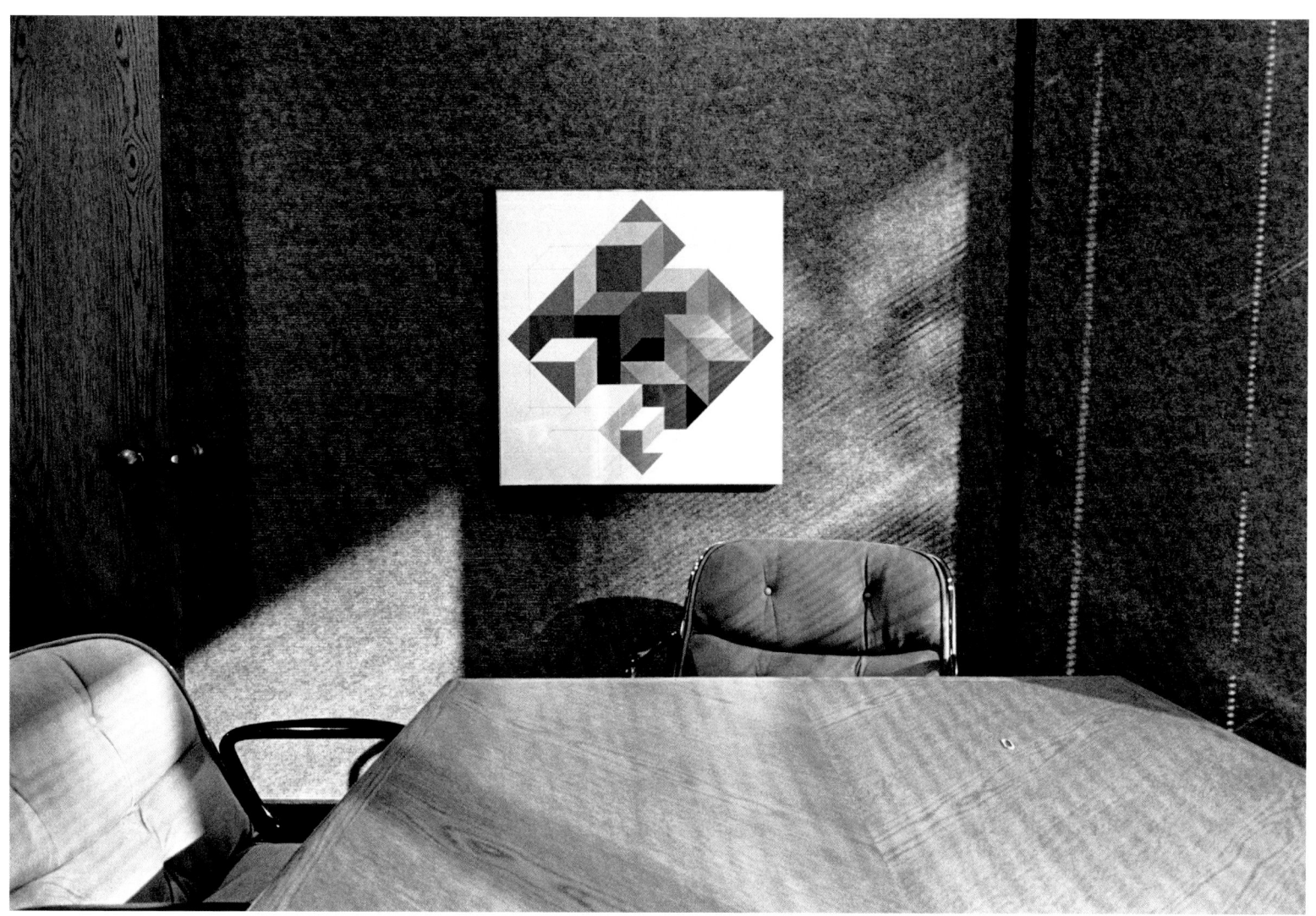

Reel/Grobman and Associates
(from the Los Angeles Documentary Project)

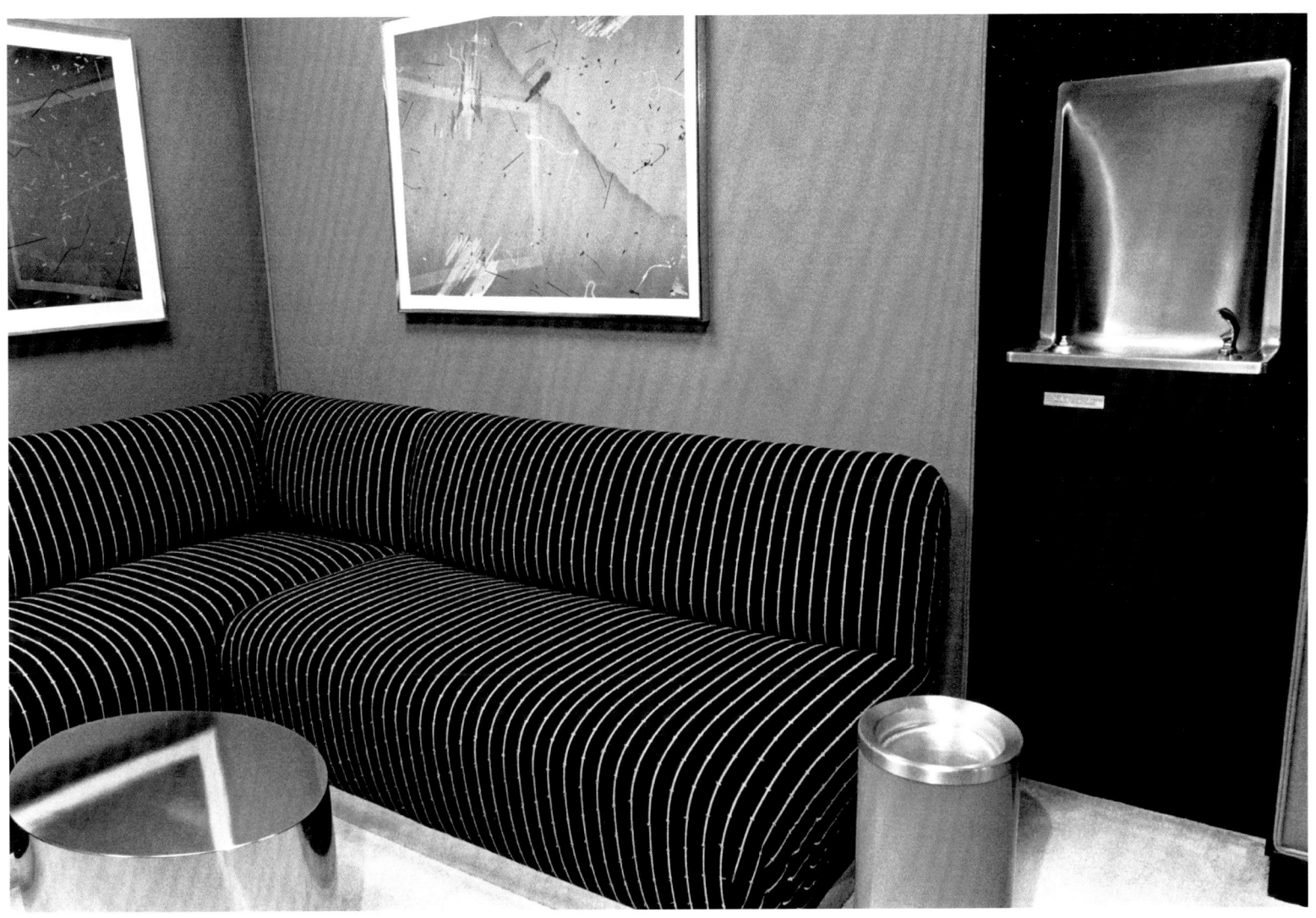

Architectural Digest
(from the Los Angeles Documentary Project)

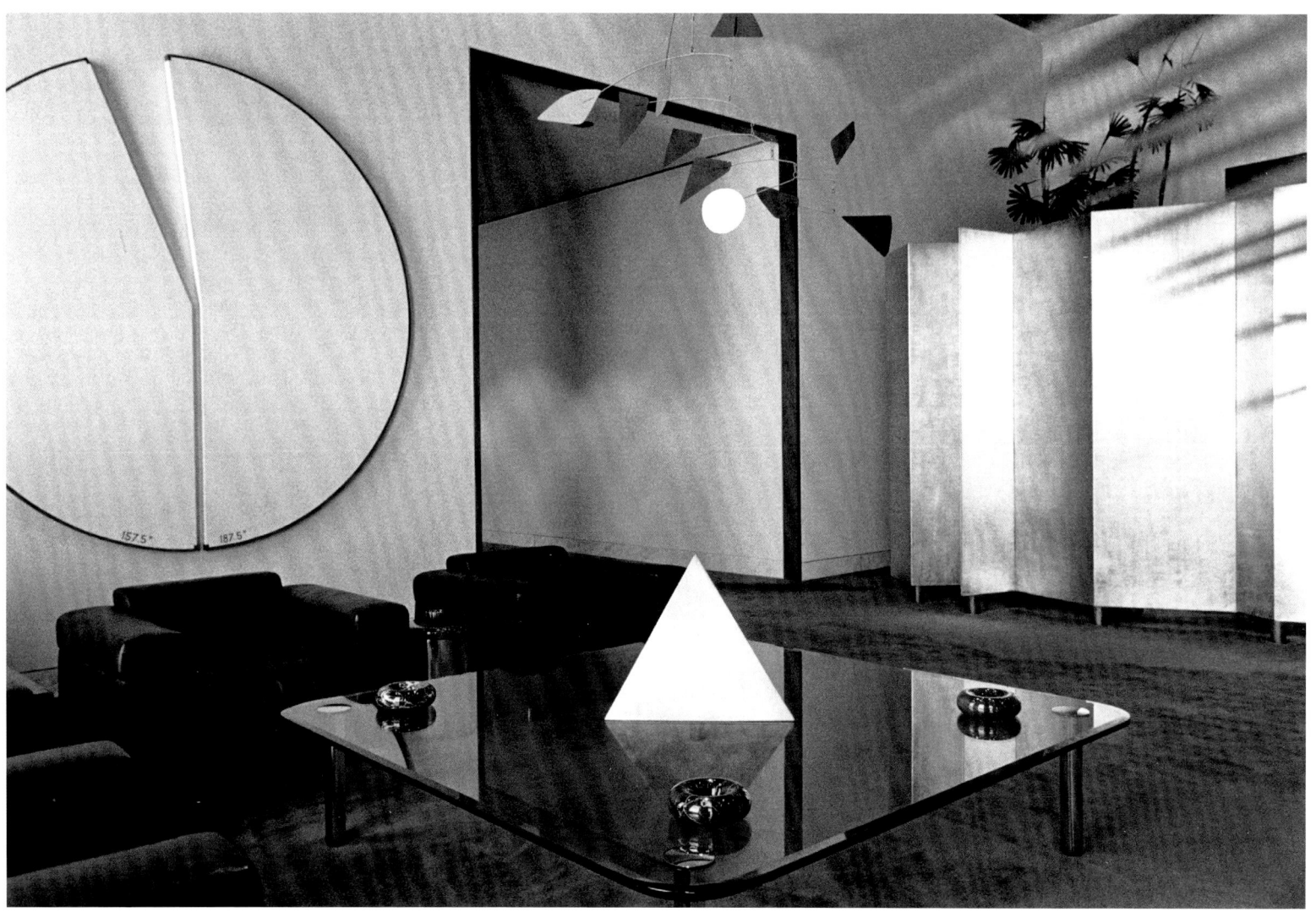

Atlantic Richfield Company (ARCO)
(from the Los Angeles Documentary Project)

Chrome

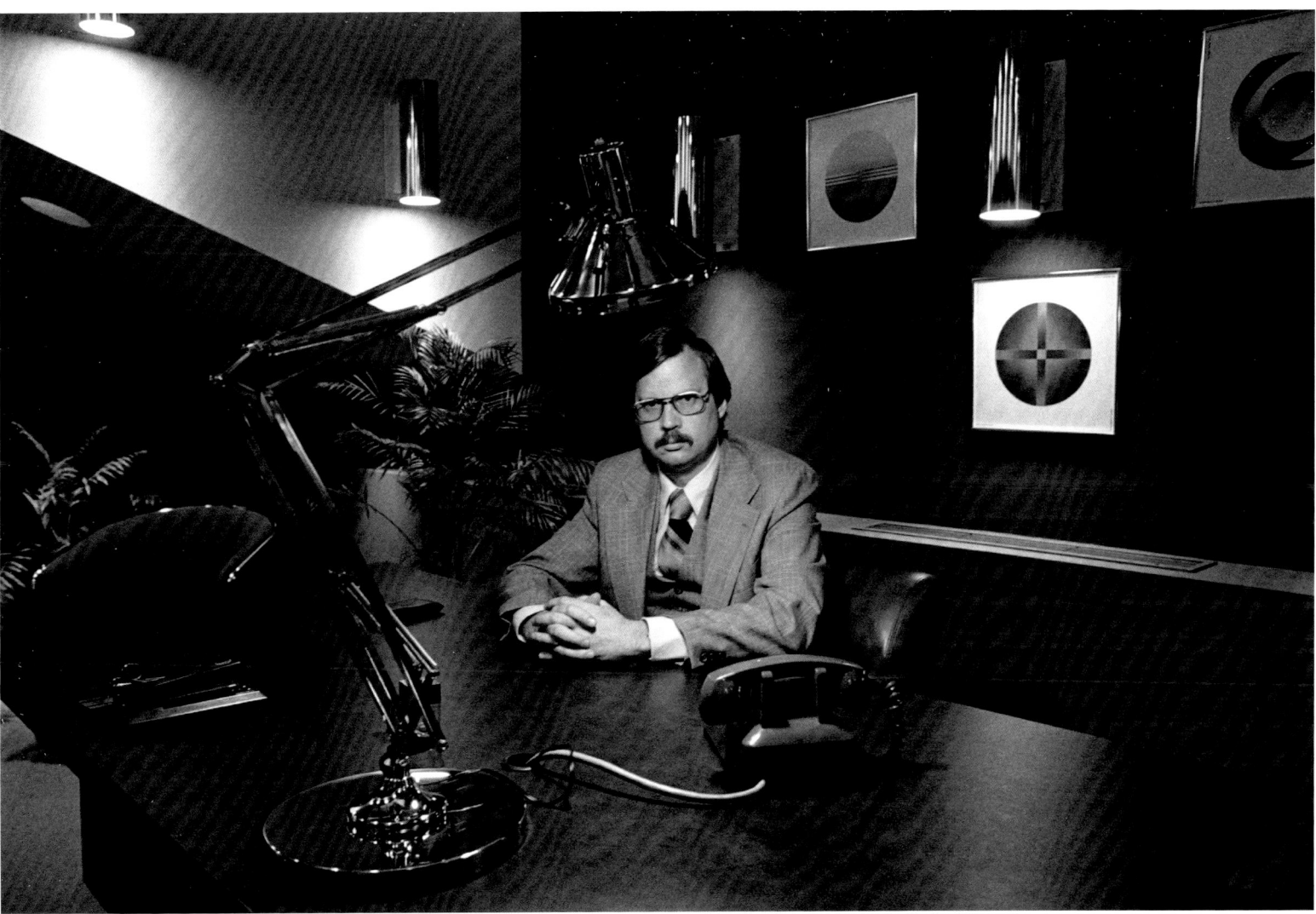

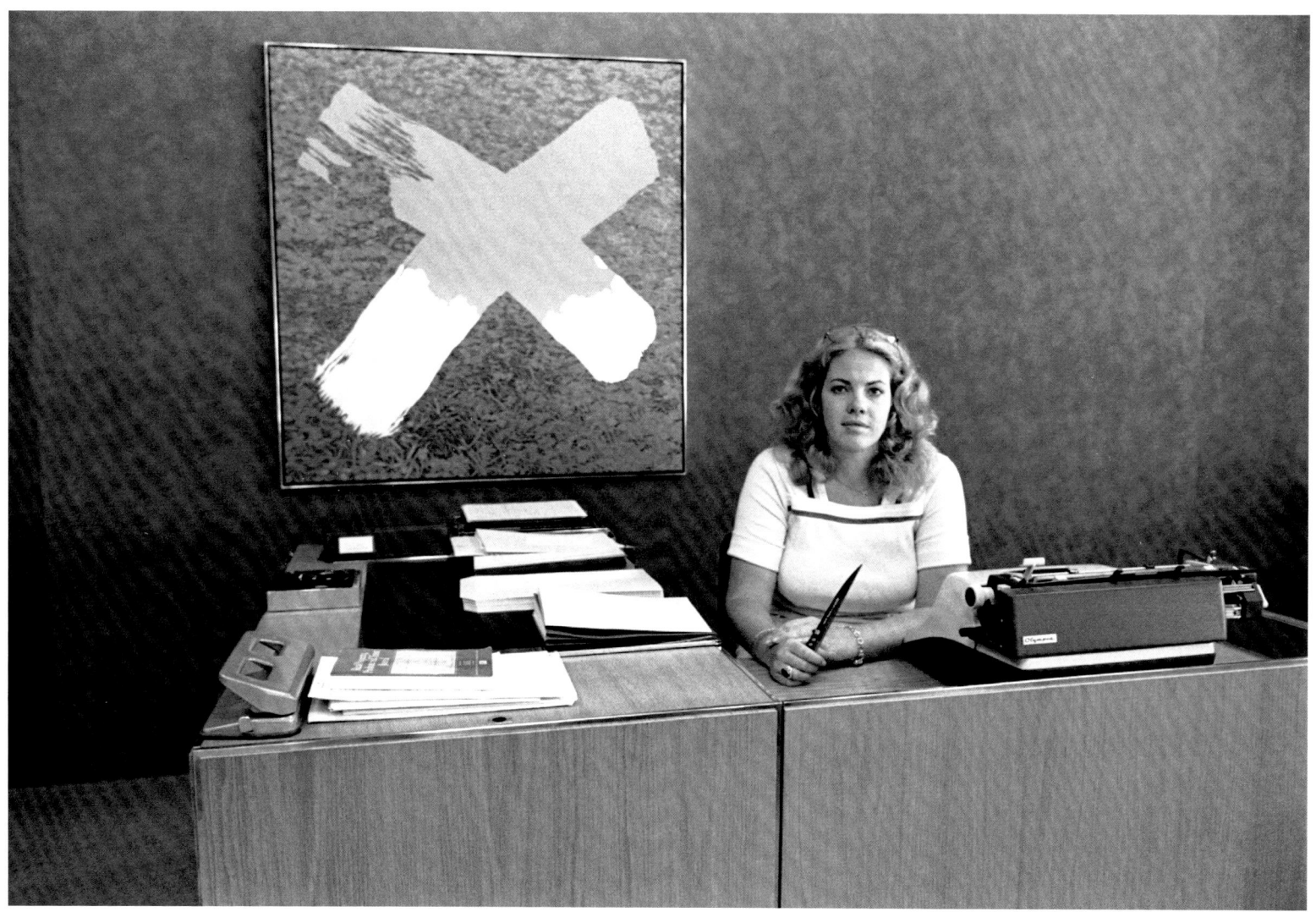

Olympia

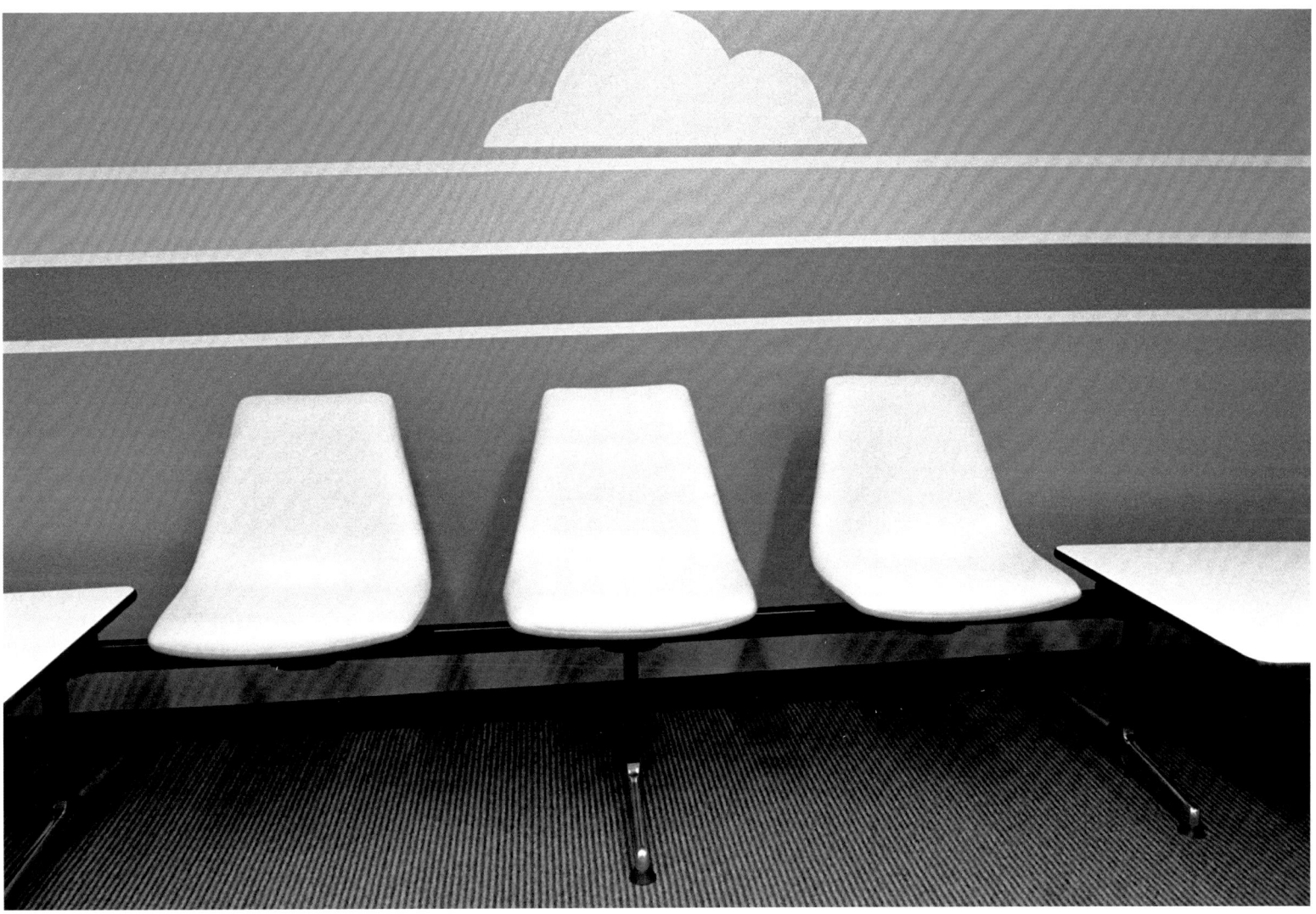

Cloud Break

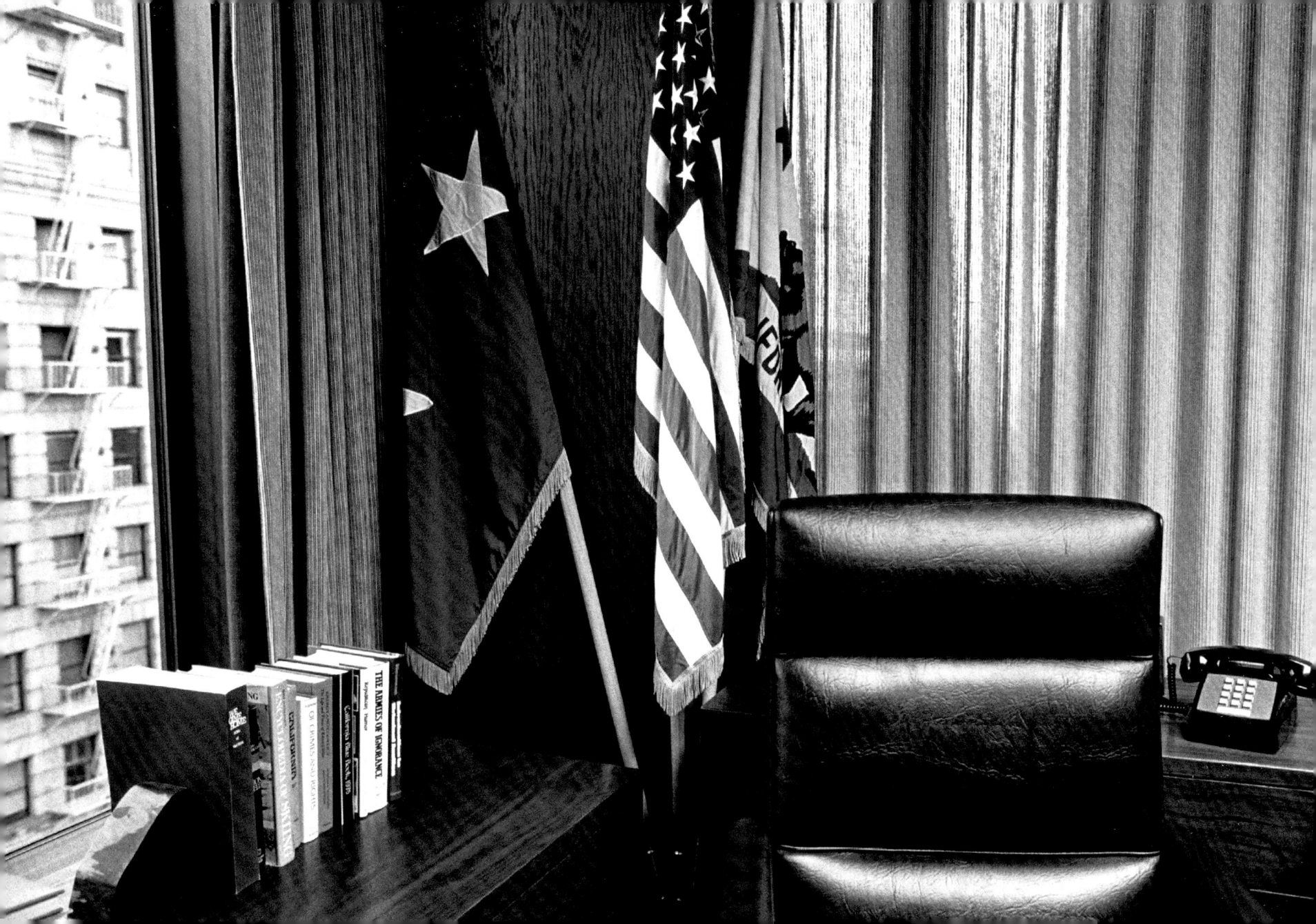

The Armies of Ignorance

Riding High

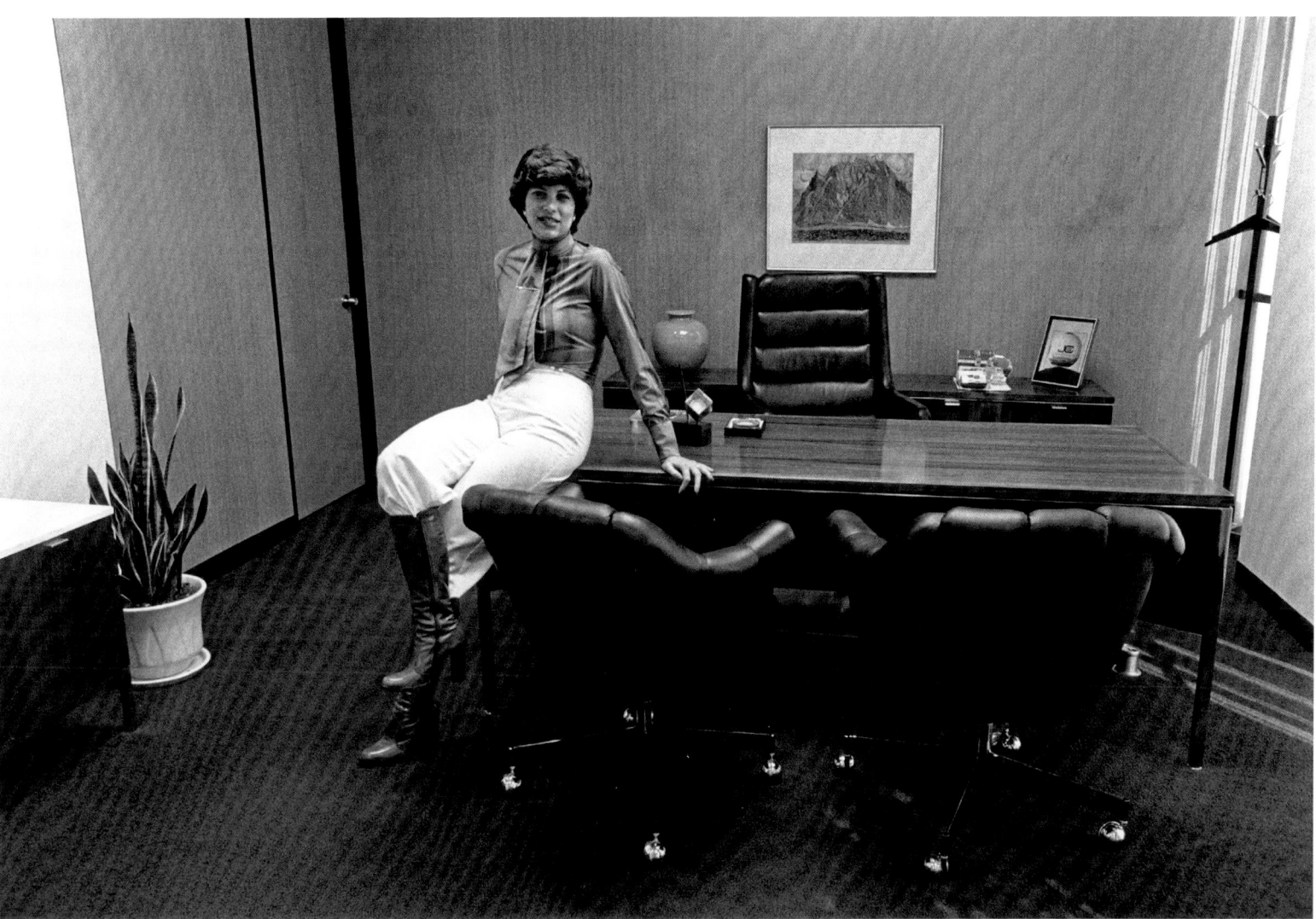

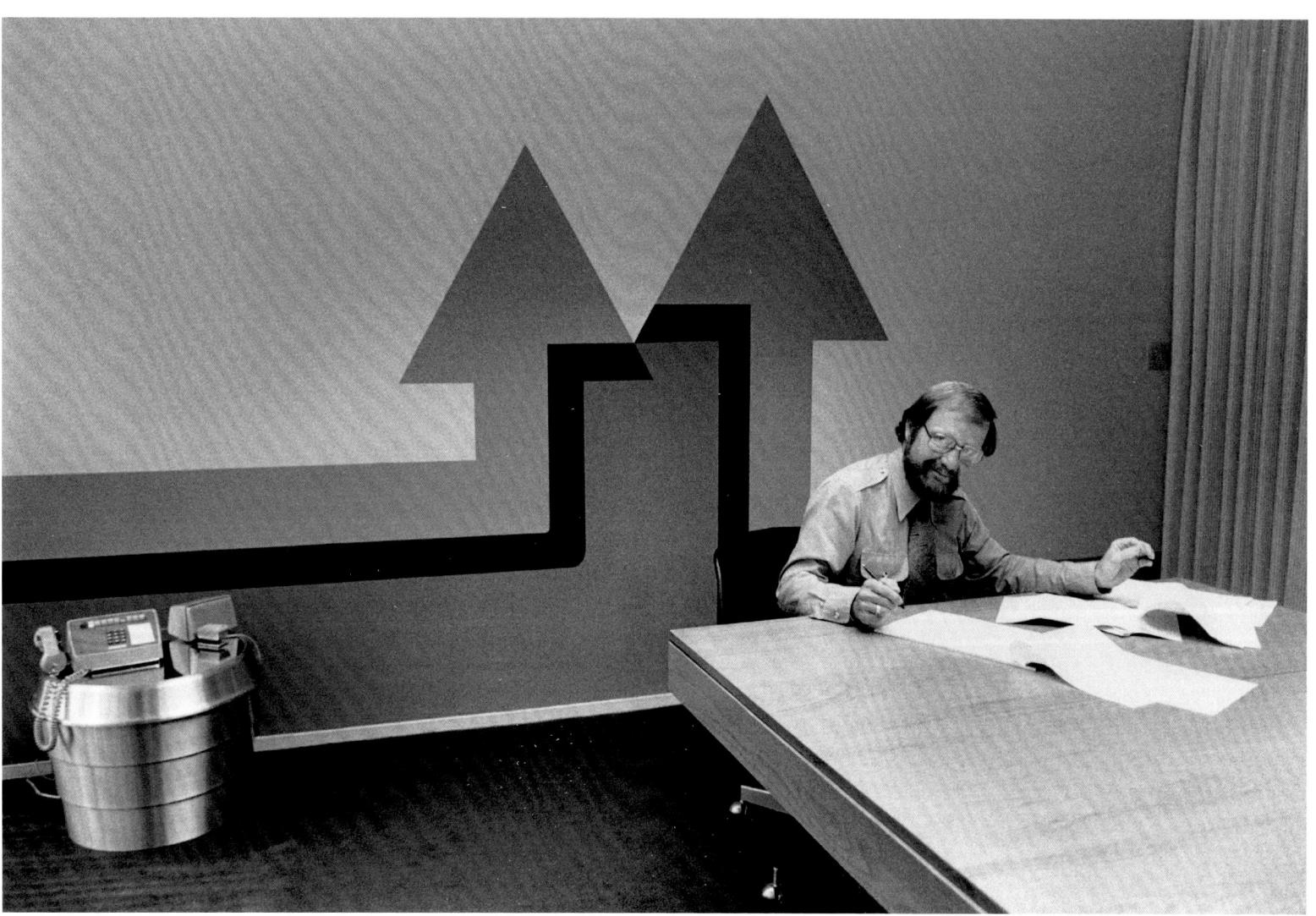

Brushed

Console

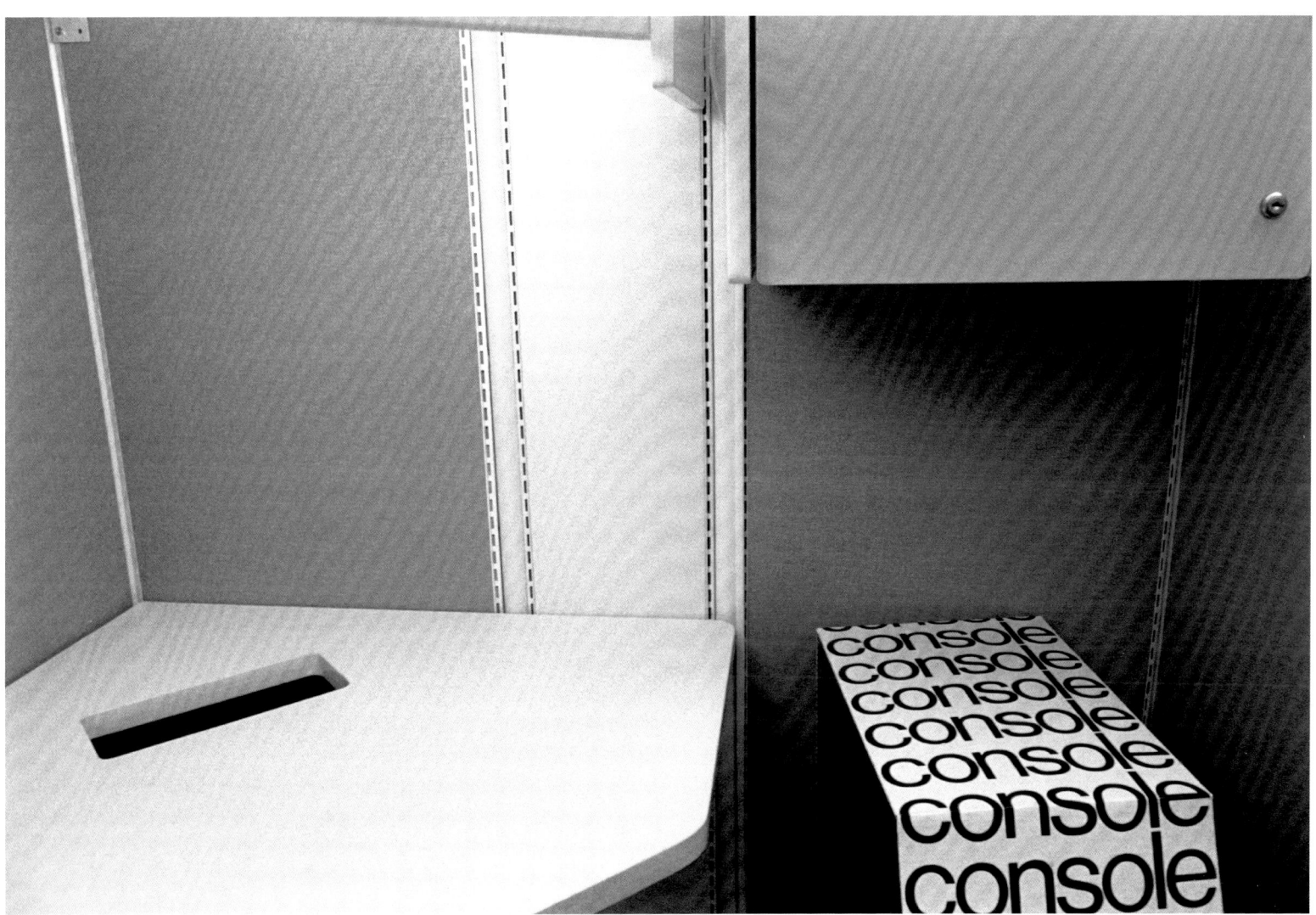

Blinds

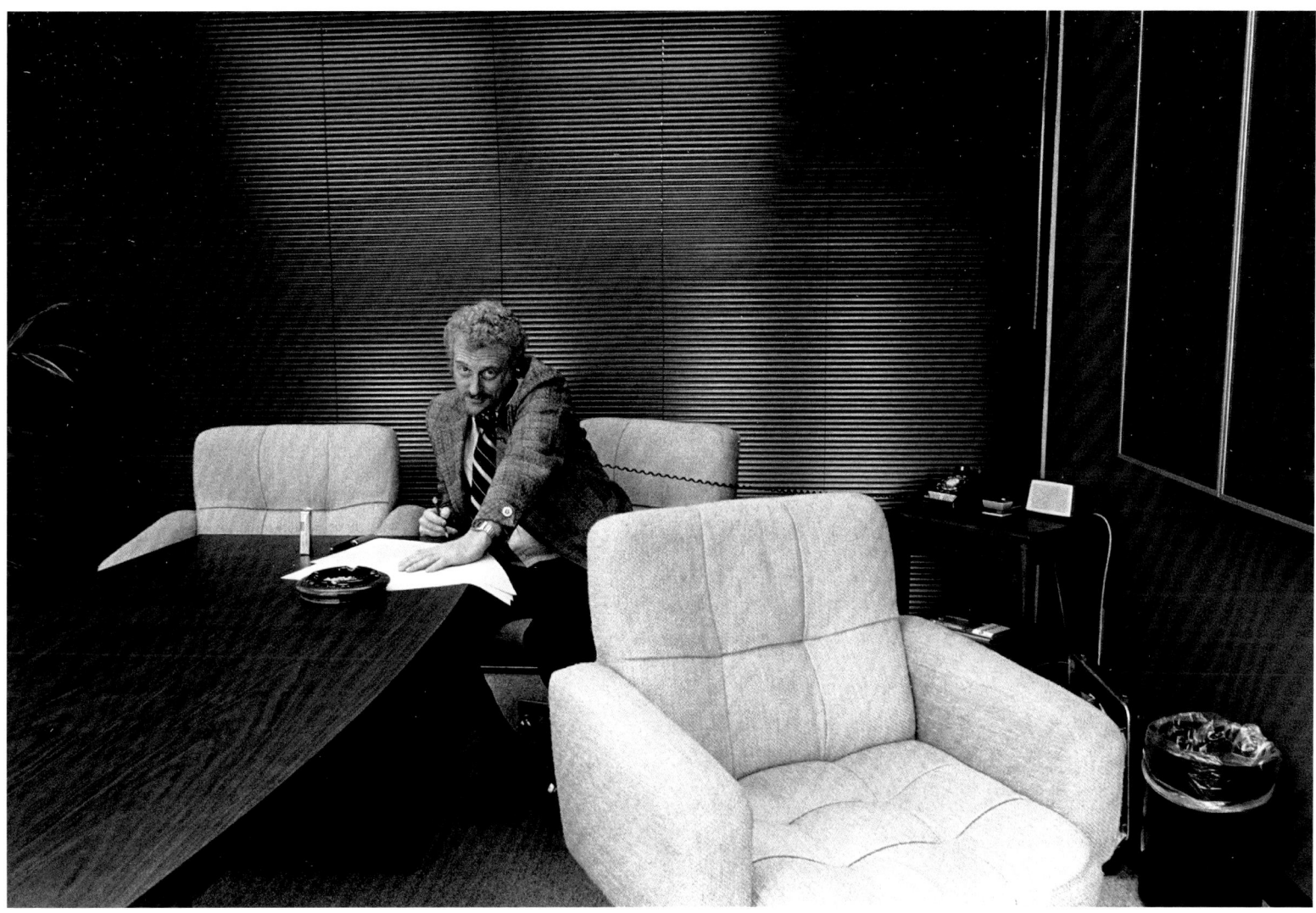

Secretary

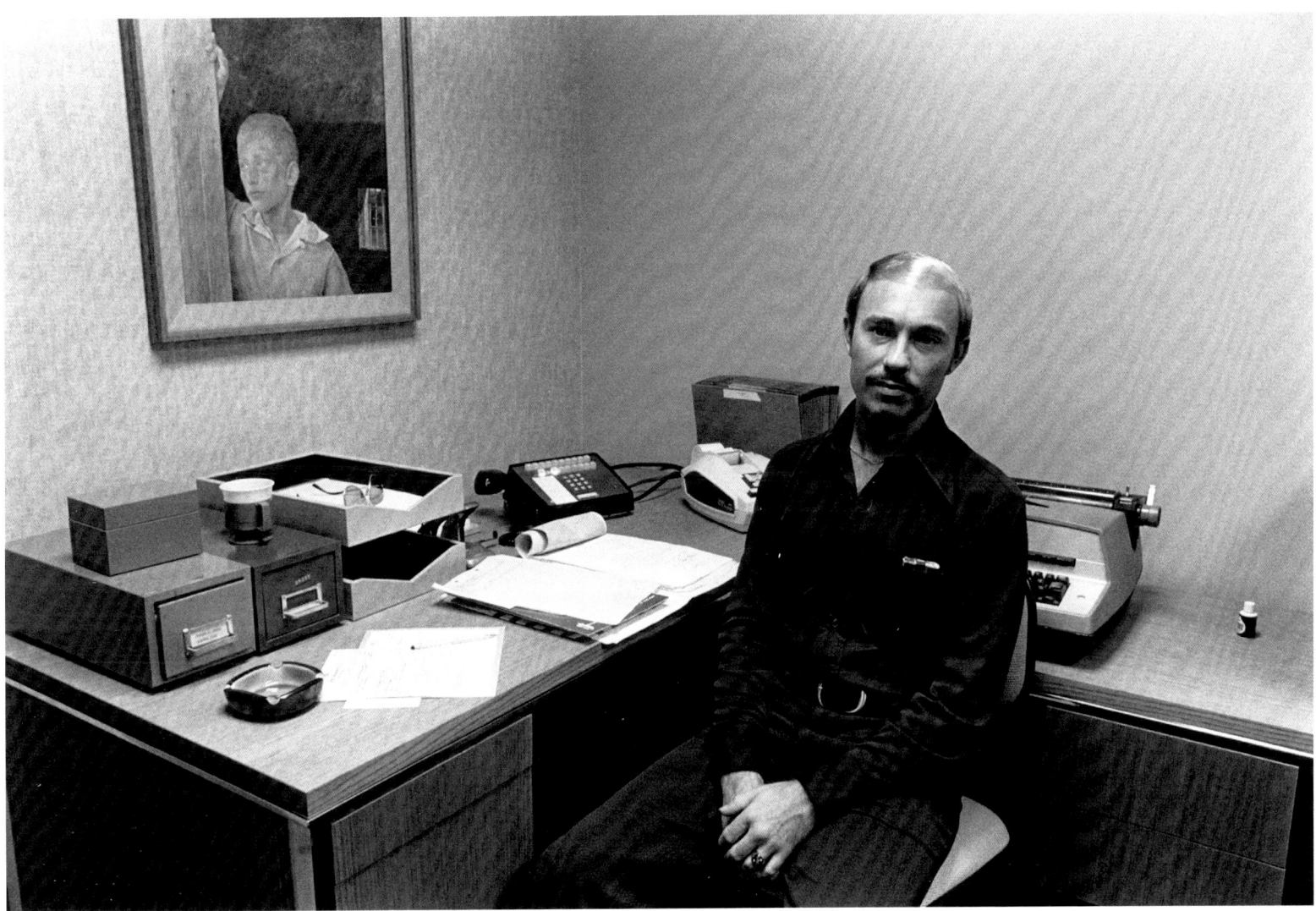

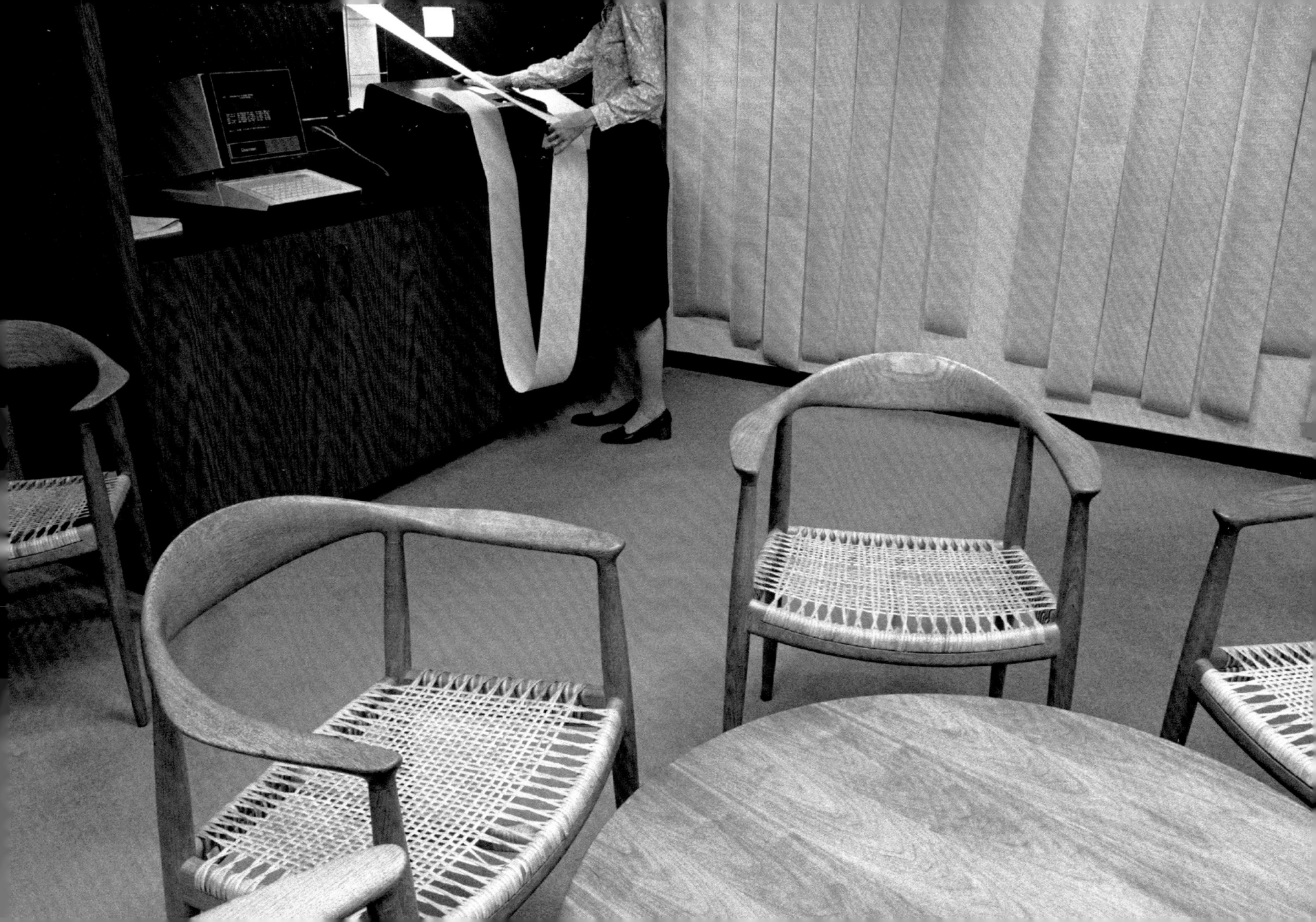

Tapes

Reflection

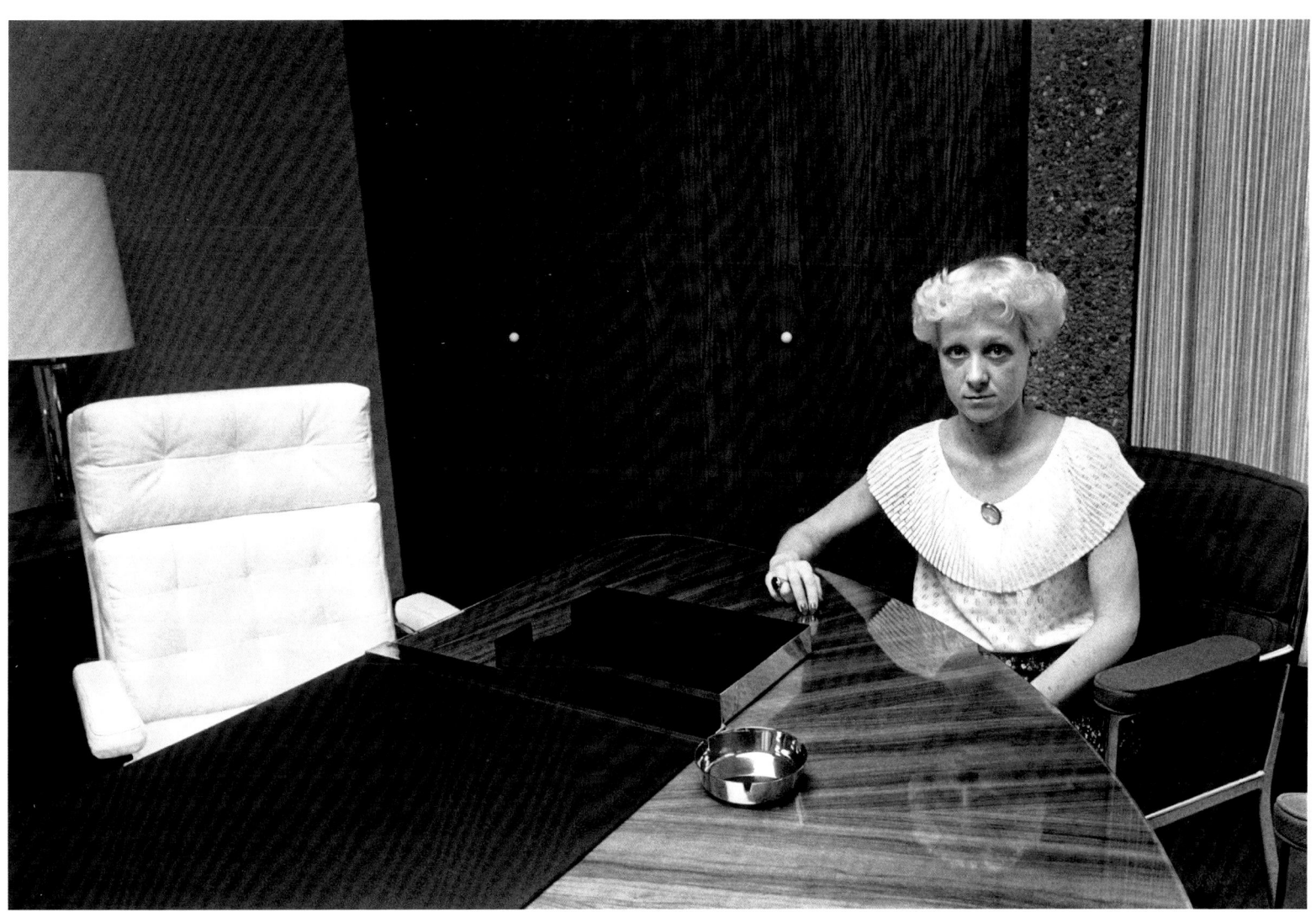

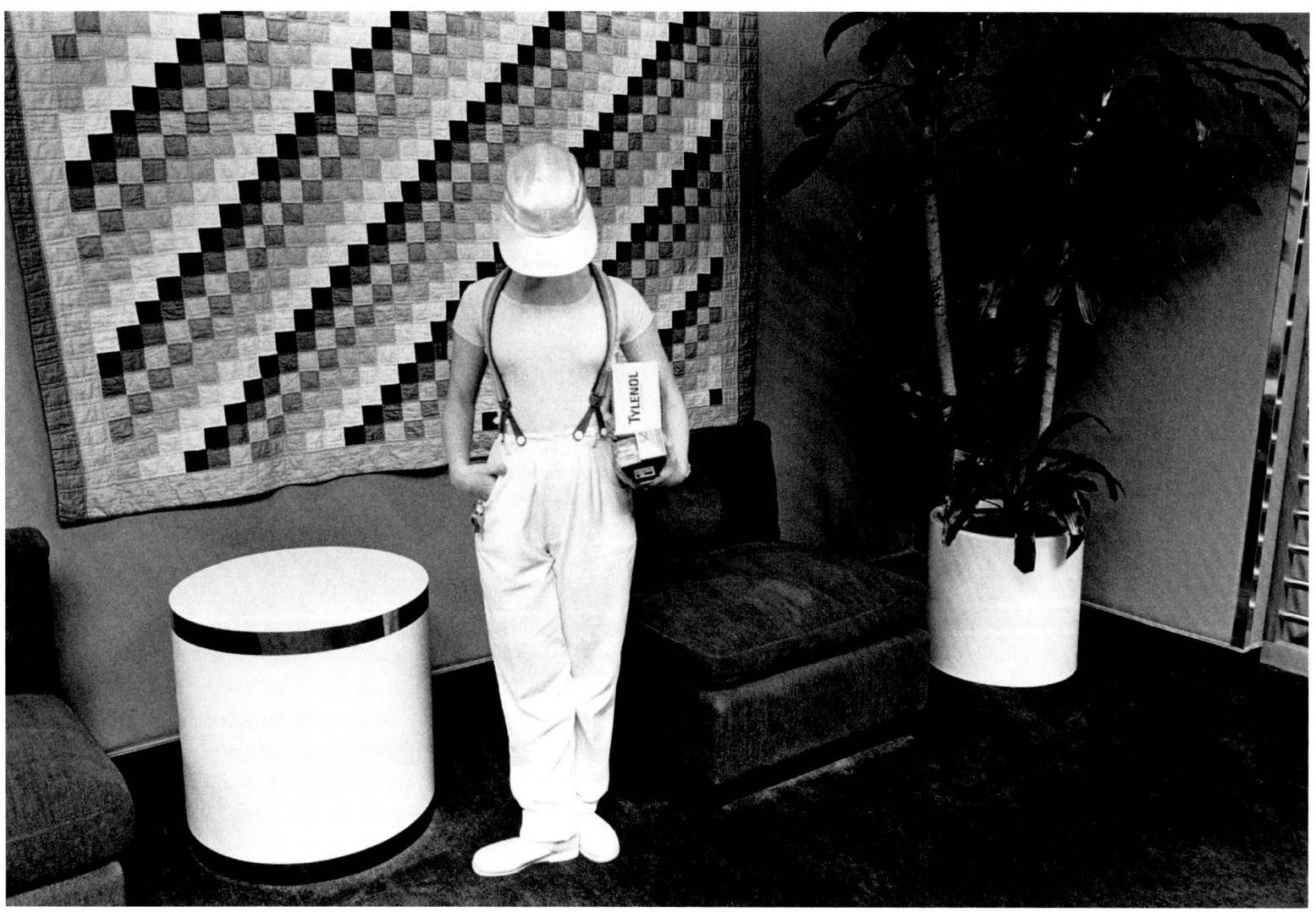

Tylenol

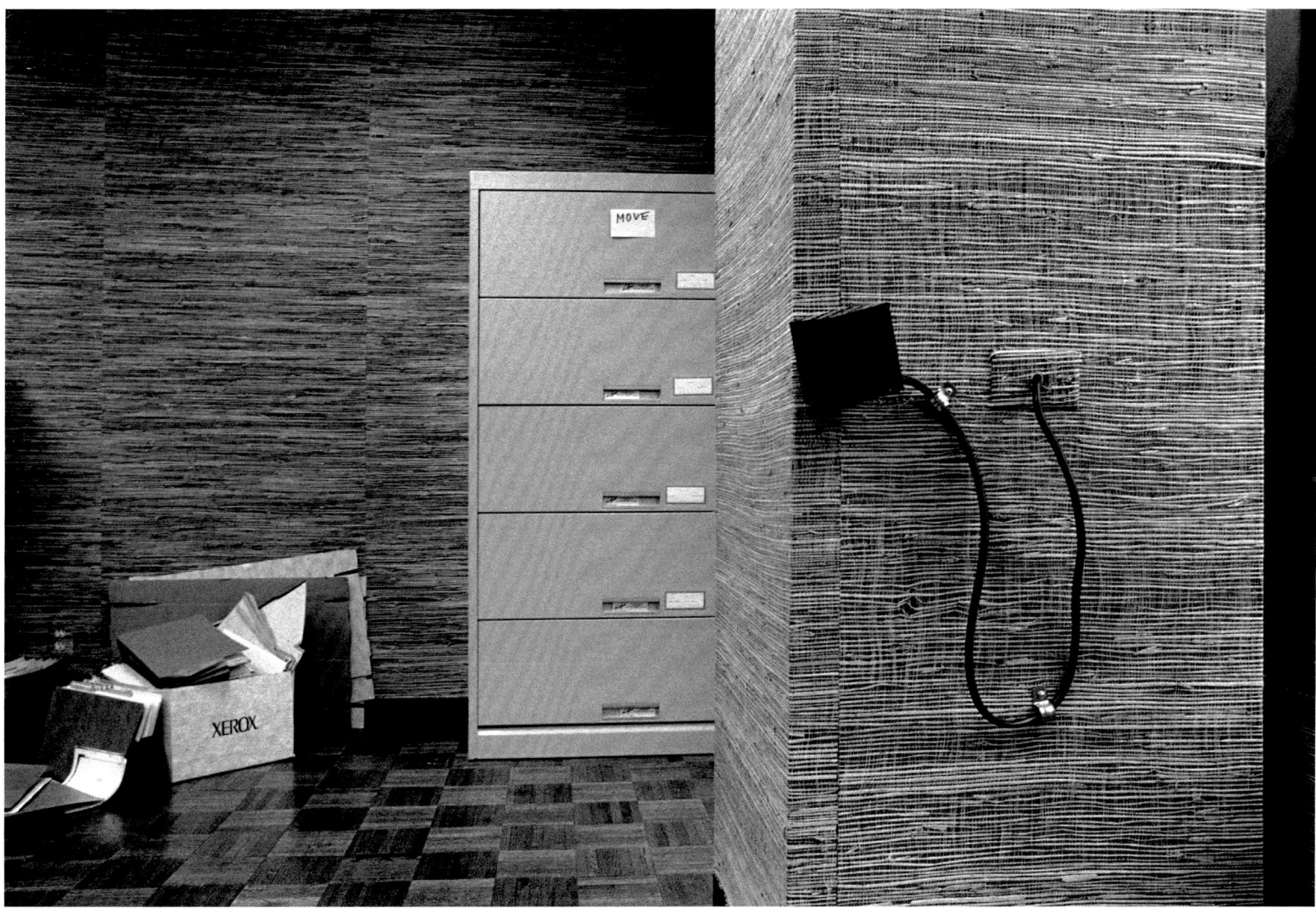

Move

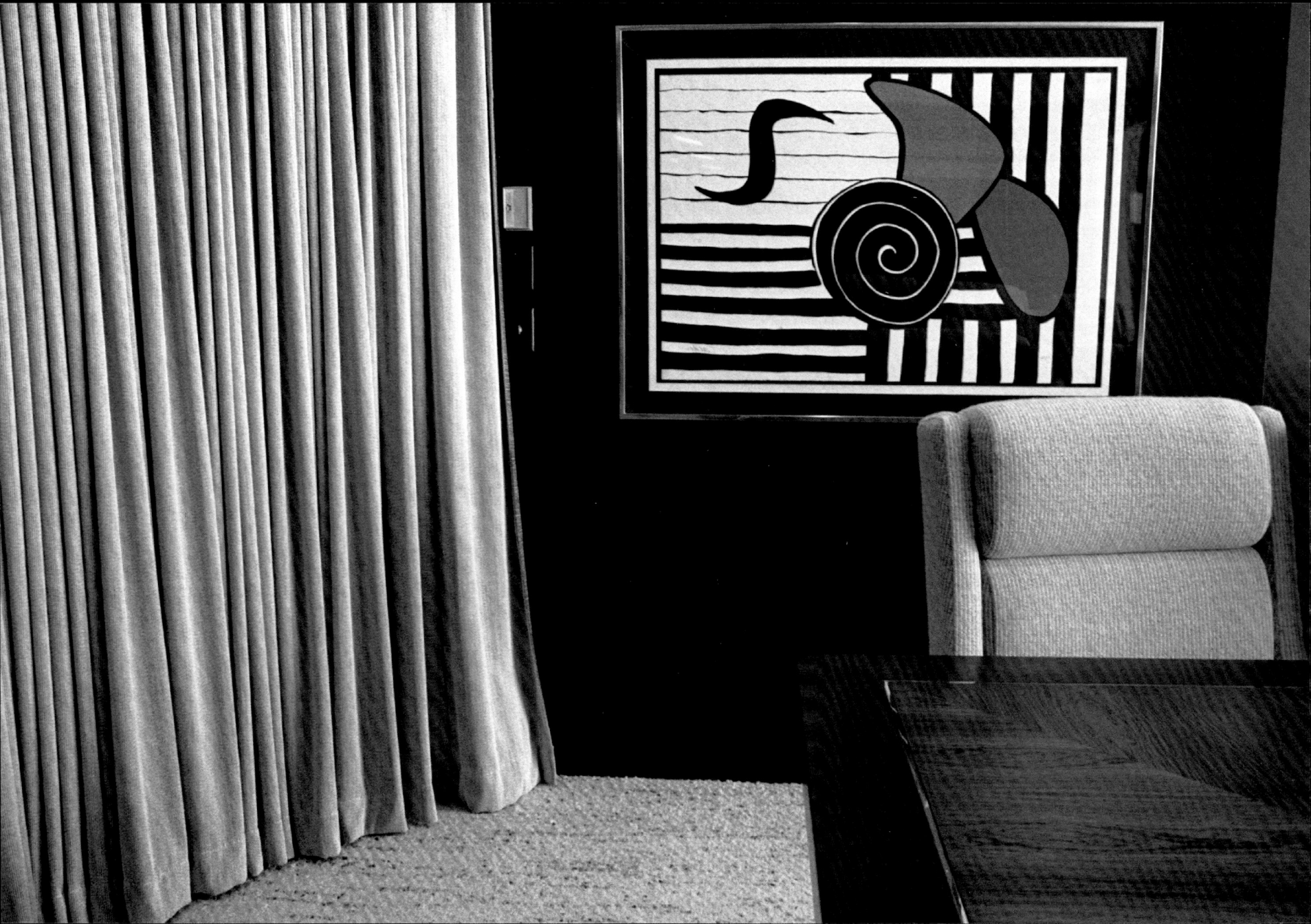

Curtains

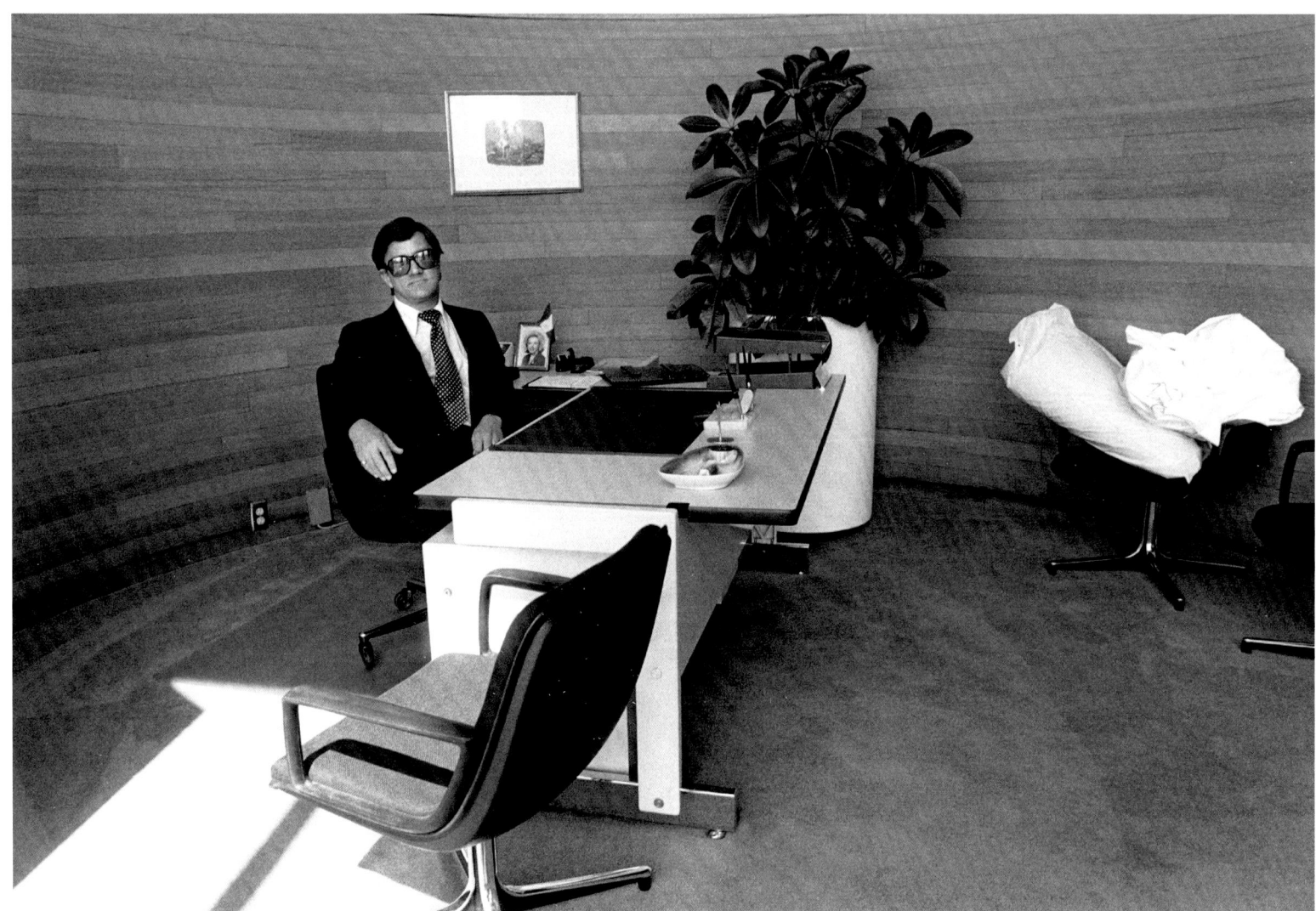

French Bank

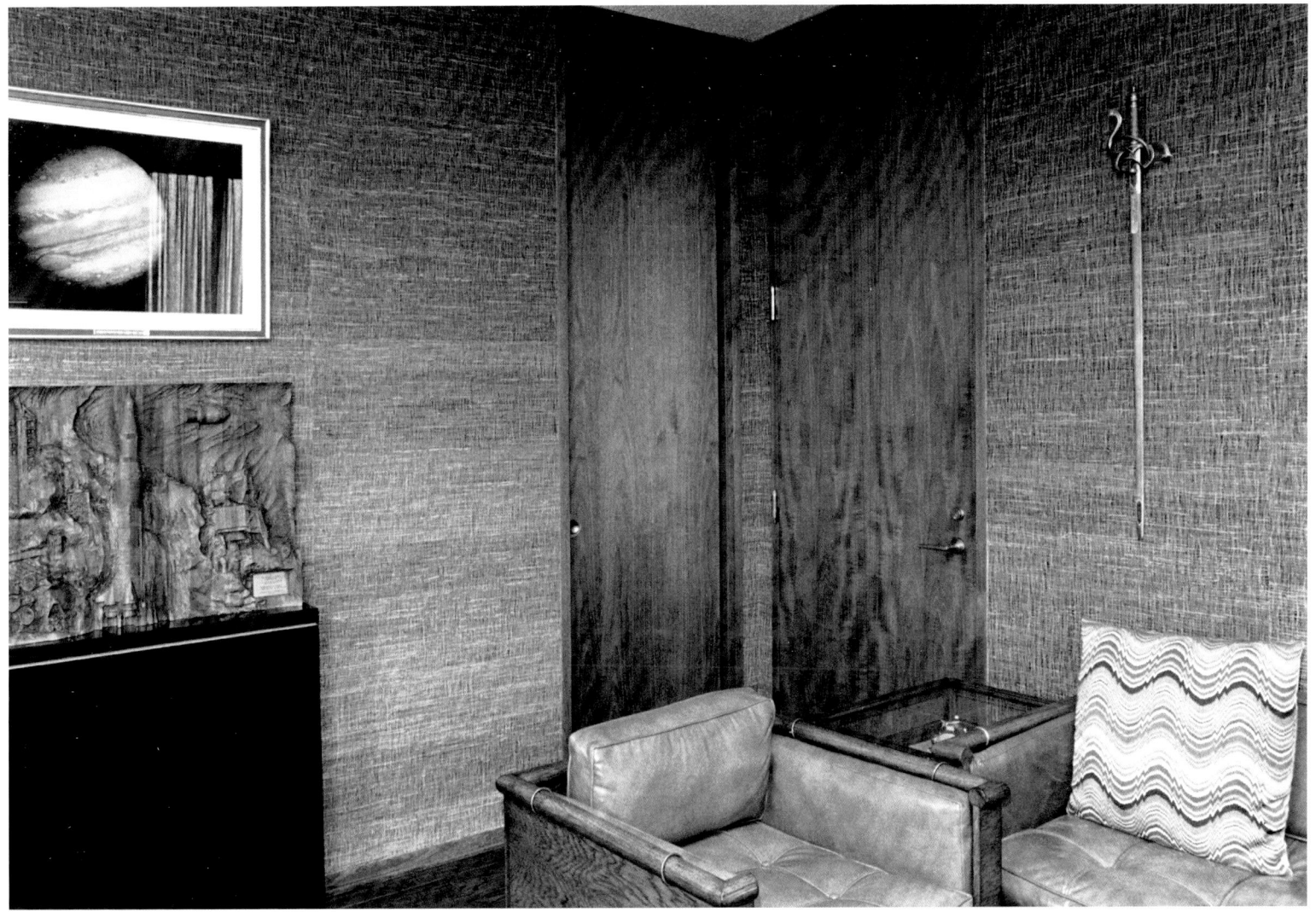

Jupiter and Sabre

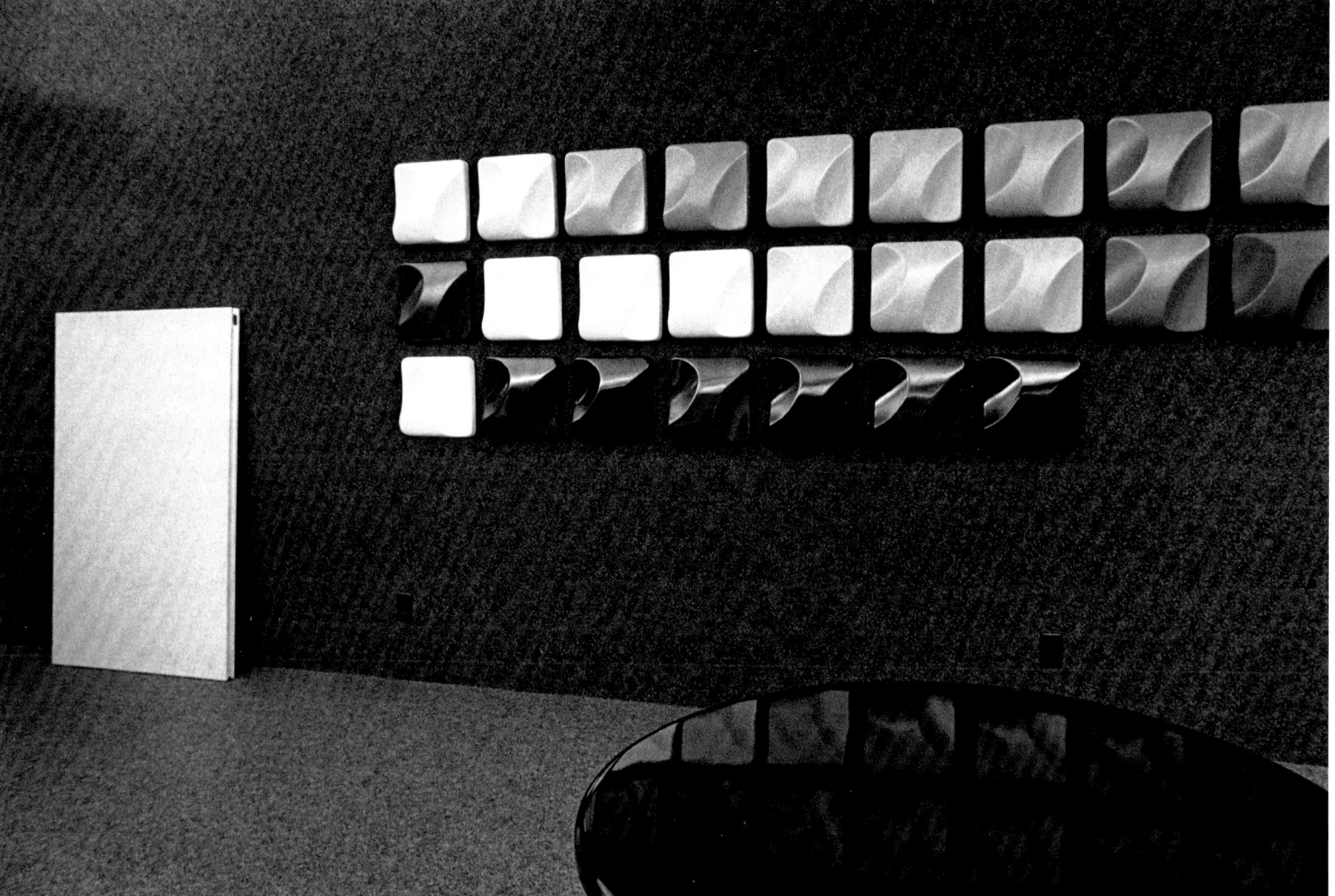

Dead

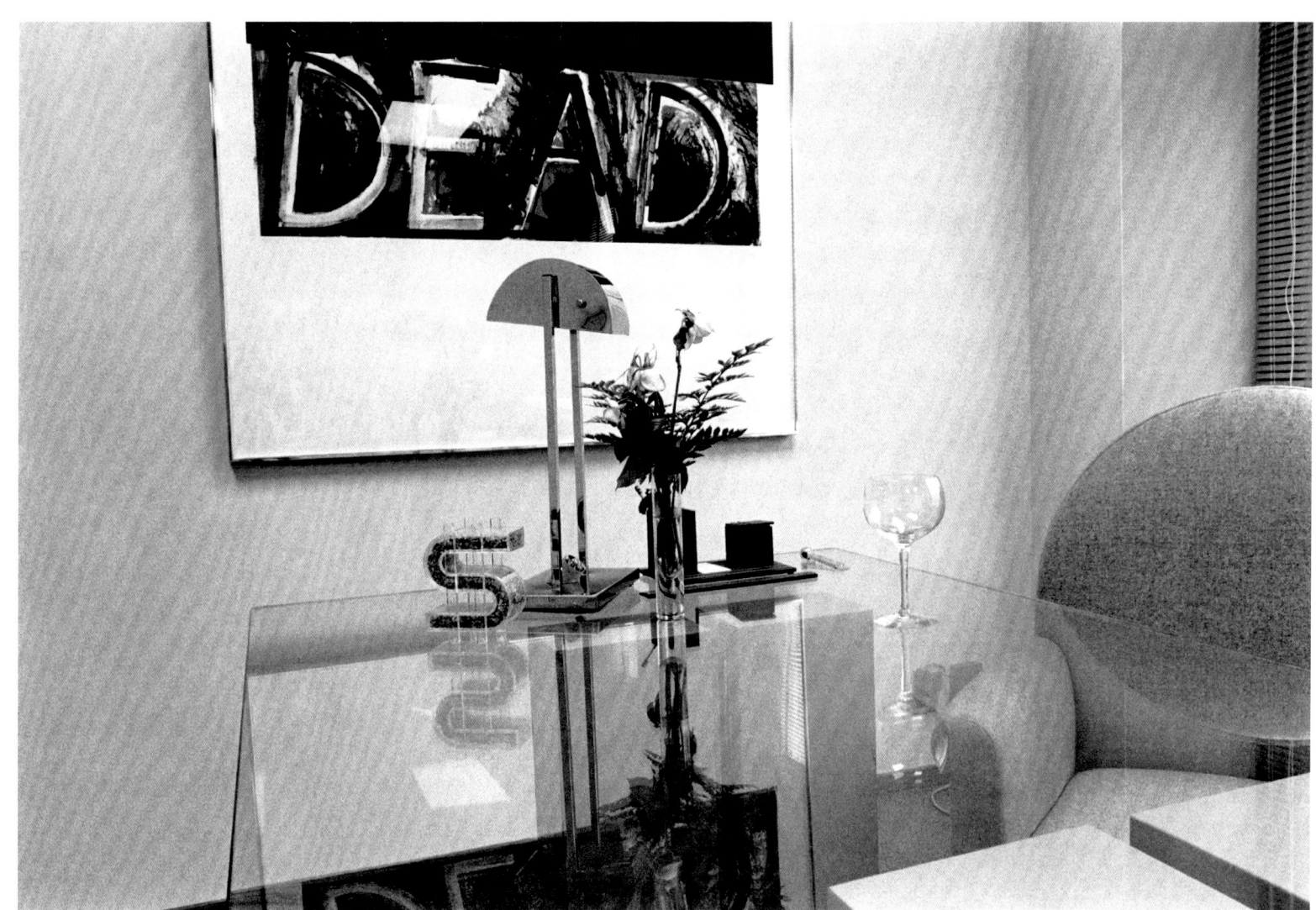

Please Ring Bell for Service

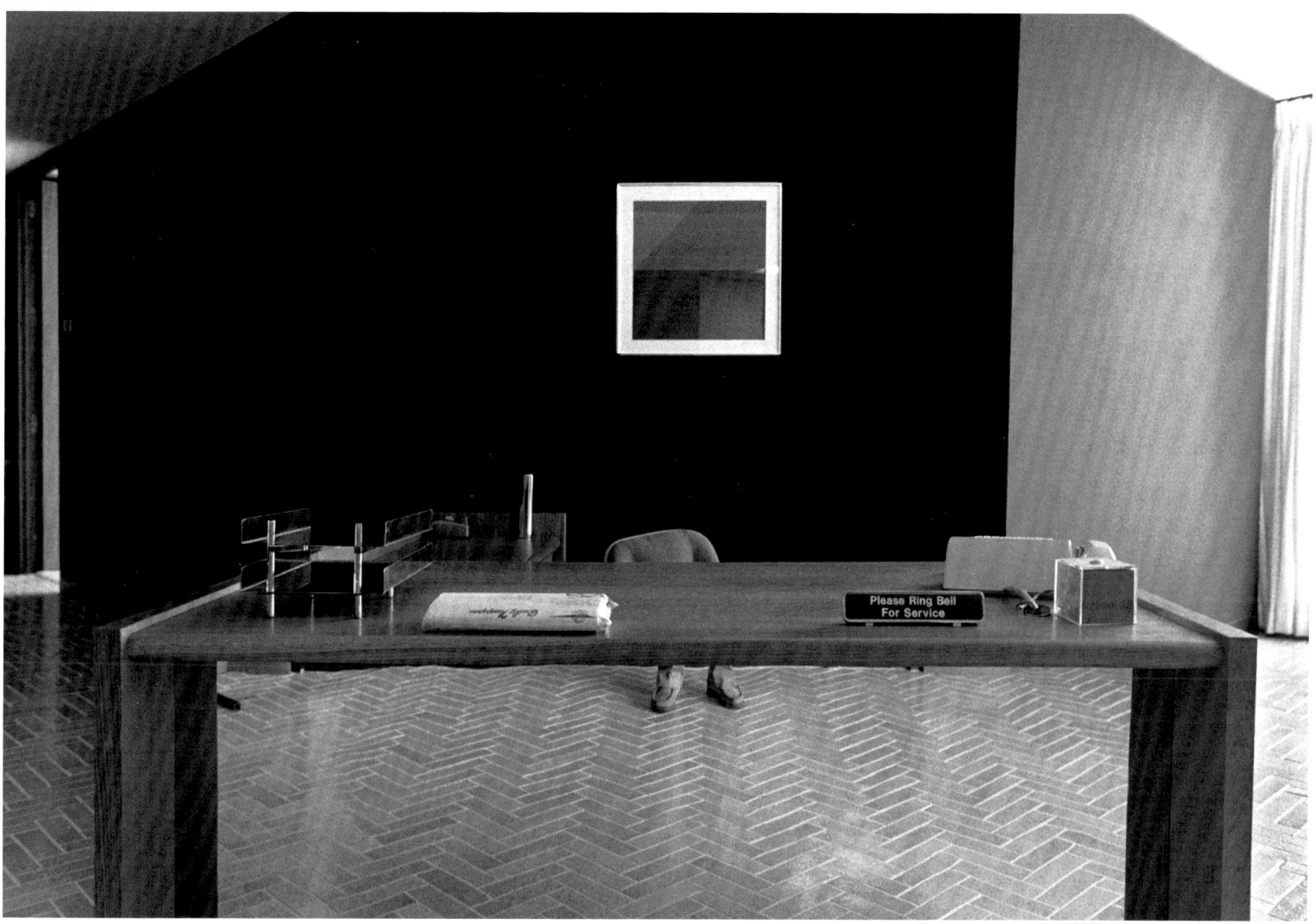

EXECUTIVE DISORDER

—Mark Rice

In *How We Got Here* (2000), David Frum plumbed the 1970s for essential truths about contemporary American life, seeing in that decade the engines of economic and social transformation that, as the book's subtitle puts it, "brought [us] modern life—for better or worse." Frum called the 1970s "a time of unease and despair, punctuated by disaster."[1] He was writing in the waning days of the twentieth century, with Bill Clinton in the White House and a fog of unease and nostalgia misting the land. But if he was worried about the state of American life in 2000, he is even more concerned now in 2017.

In the years since his book was published, the country has endured the terrorist attacks of September 11, 2001, two seemingly interminable wars, a financial meltdown that brought into stark relief the privileging of the financial sector by the federal government, the emergence of both left-wing (Occupy) and right-wing (Tea Party) populist movements in response to political, social, and economic unease, and a rise in racial tensions. Perhaps most importantly, the country has installed Donald Trump in the White House. Frum's cover story of the March 2017 issue of *The Atlantic*, "How to Build an Autocracy," spells out how the Trump administration could lead the United States away from liberal democracy. Widely read and widely admired, Frum grimly assesses the current political situation, seeing in Trump threats to American life that are perhaps unlike any encountered in the past.

I open with Frum's analyses of contemporary American life in order to draw attention to the fact that Susan Ressler's collection of photographs, *Executive Order*, comes at an opportune time. Her images of corporate America were made in the mid to late 1970s and provide a glimpse inside a rising economic order as they reveal the reception rooms and inner sancta of premier corporate office spaces. They were made at a pivotal point both in the postindustrial shifts of the American economy

---

[1] David Frum, *How We Got Here: The 70's: The Decade that Brought You Modern American Life—For Better or Worse* (New York: Basic Books, 2000), xxiii.

and in American photography, when a younger generation of photographers grappled with questions of aesthetics and epistemologies. By bringing these photos to audiences now, Ressler provides viewers new ways of understanding the worlds of photography and American corporate culture as they intersected in her lens during the decade that brought us "modern life." It's all here—upstart technology companies, defense contractors, law firms, financial firms, the film and music industries, and so on, and the economies of power, consumption, and leisure. Ressler reveals many of the absurdities and pomposities that inhere in corporate America in her photographs, and they, like Frum's book, draw our attention to how we came to be where we are today.

I first encountered Ressler's photographs about twenty years ago. I was nearing the end of graduate school, in that heady and nerve-wracking phase of figuring out just how I was going to be able to complete a doctoral dissertation about American photography in the 1970s. In that dissertation, which became my first book, *Through the Lens of the City: NEA Photography Surveys of the 1970s*, I told the story of a mostly forgotten documentary grant category established and maintained in

the second half of the 1970s by the National Endowment for the Arts.

There were two main goals for the NEA Photography Survey grant category: to record American life and simultaneously to link documentary photography to fine art photography. Emerging in the 1970s bicentennial era, the surveys reflected a widespread interest in taking stock of American life at that particular moment in time, through photographic explorations of specific neighborhoods, of cities large and small, and of whole states. The idea was that such projects would accumulate into a portrait of a rapidly changing nation. From this perspective, the surveys were simultaneously nostalgic and forward-looking, an apt combination for a nation uneasy both about its history and about the prospects for its future.

In addition, the NEA surveys attempted to bridge the gap between photography operating in the documentary tradition and photography as a fine art. The 1970s represent a high-water mark in the history of American photography in terms of the practice, theory, criticism, and acceptance of photography as a fine art. Photographs began to find their way into museums and gallery spaces formerly off-limits to what was perceived as a "mechanical" art form. That the National Endowment for the Arts, the very name of which signifies its commitment to art, created a separate grant category that self-consciously called attention to the utility of the camera for recording the natural, social, and built environments reveals something about the conversations taking place about what photography does and how it goes about recording, revealing, representing, and reflecting the world.

The size and scope of the surveys varied, and Ressler was a participant in one of the largest and most ambitious of the surveys: the Los Angeles Documentary Project (1979–80). She was selected to participate "on the basis of [her] familiarity with Los Angeles and on the strengths of [the] documentary work" that she had already completed, both in Los Angeles and in other cities of the American West and Southwest.[2] She coordinated her activities with seven other photographers, each working in their own styles and focusing on the dimensions of L.A. life that struck them as most significant. In some ways, the

Los Angeles Documentary Project can be seen as a microcosm of 1970s American photography as a whole: Max Yavno worked in a traditional vein of documentary street photography in the city's ethnic neighborhoods; Joe Deal employed his "New Topographic" elevated vantage point to examine new housing and suburban sprawl; Bill Owens recorded quirky scenes that echoed the playful spirit of his earlier book, *Suburbia*; and Robbert Flick worked in a conceptual format of grids of 35mm contact prints emphasizing mobility.

While these other survey photographers worked mostly outdoors, Ressler took her camera into the lobbies and offices of the city's recently redeveloped downtown. There, she found a variety of signifiers of the new American economy: symbols of class, gender, and racial hierarchies in the physical spaces and in the people who, though mostly unseen, are very much present in her photographs. Her fifteen-print portfolio for the project, titled "The Capital Group" (and partially included here in *Executive Order*), was part of a larger undertaking begun in the mid 1970s that also dealt with corporate culture throughout the urban West. While her earlier photographs often included people enacting typified roles in the new American economy, she eventually

[2] Quoted in Mark Rice, *Through the Lens of the City: NEA Photography Surveys of the 1970s* (Jackson: University Press of Mississippi, 2005), 161.

opted to exclude people in order to concentrate on the surface planes and symbolic objects in their offices. Both approaches have powerful effects. While the inclusion of people allows us to recognize that real human activity (in all its messy details) goes on in these sites, the removal of people allows us to focus on the hollowness at the heart of corporate America.

All of Ressler's photographs in this book return us to a moment when the American West and Southwest were in full bloom, with the rise of the so-called Sun Belt shifting the center of gravity of the American economy, politics, and population away from the Northeast to the South and the West. Energy, aerospace, and high technology were some of the main drivers of the economic shifts taking place. Corporate parks, glass-skinned high rises, and sprawling suburbs were the new boomtowns that emphasized efficiency and utility. Once inside of these buildings, one felt a sense of dislocation, as though one could be almost anywhere, insulated by the climate control and flat lighting of ultimately soulless business suites. Looking more closely at these cookie-cutter spaces, one sees efforts to make them distinctive through the selection of wall hangings, furniture styles, and the various totems of success that the rich

and powerful surround themselves with. Look more closely still, and the emptiness reveals itself. Despite the efforts at grandeur, these are impermanent places, details ready to be swapped out for new ones as corporate fashions shift or as company fortunes rise and fall.

While there was plenty of gleaming construction going on in the late 1970s, there was also a serious malaise creeping across the land. In 1979, the year that Ressler's photography of office interiors reached their peak (and when the Los Angeles Documentary Project commenced), the country was in a funk. The economy was sputtering along at a dismal pace, hamstrung by a fuel crisis brought on by a revolution in Iran that by year's end would see fifty-two Americans taken hostage. Inflation was running at 13 percent. Unemployment was at 6 percent and was heading higher. The hangover of Watergate still affected the country. Many of the nation's cities were grappling with crime, homelessness, addiction, and crippling budget deficits.

In the middle of that dismal year, President Jimmy Carter, sitting behind his desk in the Oval Office, went on the air and gave what became his best-known speech to the American people, the so-called Crisis of Confidence speech. Reaching out to his fellow citizens, he asked for their help to combat what he saw as a threat creeping over the land, a threat manifested in declining faith in the country's future and the country's leaders:

> The threat is nearly invisible in ordinary ways. It is a crisis of confidence. It is a crisis that strikes at the very heart and soul and spirit of our national will. We can see this crisis in the growing doubt about the meaning of our own lives and in the loss of a unity of purpose for our Nation. . . . The erosion of our confidence in the future is threatening to destroy the social and the political fabric of America.

He went on to note that some of what ailed the nation were the changing relationships among citizenship, work, and consumption:

> In a nation that was proud of hard work, strong families, close-knit communities, and our faith in God, too many of us now tend to worship self-indulgence and consumption. Human identity is no longer defined by what one does, but by what one owns. But we've discovered that owning things and consuming things does not satisfy our longing for meaning. We've learned that piling up material goods cannot fill the emptiness of lives which have no confidence or purpose.

This last point, underscored by Carter's speech, amplifies the significance of Ressler's project. For while it is true that in the late 1970s there were still hardworking, close-knit families, and while it is true that even before the 1970s there were plenty of people who worshipped consumption, a shift in the prominence of each in the cultural imagination had taken place. The yeoman was being replaced by the yuppie.

The cultural crises and economic shifts of the 1970s have caught the attention of many historians who share Ressler's (and Frum's) interest in "how we got here." Take for example, Judith Stein's book, *Pivotal Decade*, the main argument of which is spelled out in her chosen subtitle: *How the United States Traded Factories for Finance in the Seventies*. In a similar vein, Jefferson Cowie's, *Stayin' Alive: The 1970s and the Last Days of the Working Class*, closely examines the economic transformations and dislocations of the 1970s. Cowie notes that Carter's "Crisis of Confidence" speech gave the president a short-lived bump in approval ratings by American voters. By 1980, however, it had become clear to increasing numbers of Americans that Carter was not the one to restore confidence in American life. That would fall to Ronald Reagan, a self-styled outsider candidate for president who argued for a limitless future if only the economy could be unshackled, an argument that Donald Trump echoes more than thirty years later. Then, as now, the fat cats were led to the trough to feed at the expense of working-class Americans. "After Reagan's inaugural address" in 1981, Cowie writes, "Washington descended into an unprecedented orgy of conspicuous consumption as the richest of the rich returned to power."[3] In the ensuing years, the wages of most Americans would stagnate. The rich, on the other hand, just kept getting richer.

What do these books and Carter's speech have to do with Ressler's work? While some photographers in the 1970s, such as Chauncey Hare and his scathing indictment of power elites in *Interior America*, focused their cameras on the lives of blue-collar workers, Ressler was attuned to the changing economic landscape and so chose to examine the world of this escalating new economy. It was in affluent environments of excess and largesse that Ressler found and explored her tableaux to photograph. While it may appear that she just happened upon the office spaces that she photographed, the fact is that in at least some of them, she rearranged objects in order to compose the images for maximal effect. In her own words, she wanted "to pierce the armor of wealth and privilege that girds the loins of the rich in America." Describing her photograph of the corporate headquarters of Atlantic Richfield, she writes "the artifice of this interior, no matter how tasteful, is ultimately hollow." She adds in an artist statement that she used "formal geometry to construct arenas of financial power as sterile, isolating spaces . . . emblematic of consumer capitalism."[4]

In addition to the corporate culture subject matter that she photographed, it is worth considering Ressler's aesthetic decisions and methodology. For example, while she shares an affinity for photographing the interiors of public spaces with Lynne Cohen, their methodologies differ in important ways. For

---

[3] Jefferson Cowie, *Stayin' Alive: The 1970s and the Last Days of the Working Class* (New York: The New Press, 2010), 310.

[4] Susan Ressler, "Artist Statement" in self-published monograph, *Portfolio 2016.*

example, unlike Ressler, Cohen photographed her scenes just as she encountered them. Also, Cohen never included people while Ressler sometimes did. Cohen used a large-format camera and composed for symmetry and balance in scenes that frequently suggested expansive openness; Ressler shot with a 35mm camera and often composed her photographs so that one feels boxed in and claustrophobic, confined by corporate culture itself. Despite these differences, Ressler, too, conveys sentiments that L.A. curator Britt Salvesen notes about Cohen's photographs: They "speak to the present in remarkably precise terms" and allow us "to confront the mysteries of photography's relation to time: its potential to collapse past and present, its function as either aid or antidote to nostalgia, and its endowment of mundane objects with potent messages."[5]

Ressler's work shares some affinities, too, with New Topographics photography that emerged in the 1970s. Like that work, there is an undercurrent of irony and a "cool detachment"[6] in her work. However, unlike the new topographical fascination with the "man-altered" landscapes and the exterior surfaces of the built environment, Ressler took the logical (though atypical) step of moving the investigation indoors. What goes on in the shiny new skyscrapers that Nicholas Nixon photographed in Boston? What's on the inside of the boxy industrial parks that Lewis Baltz photographed in Southern California? Where do the residents of Robert Adams's Colorado front-range communities go to work? The New Topographics photographs didn't ask those questions. Ressler did.

Indeed, Ressler's photographs almost completely eliminate any views of exterior environments. To determine where one actually is, one has to look for hints in the interior: Is there a sign, a plaque, an address that might anchor this place into a particular fixed point in space? Usually there isn't, but a few photographs allow a glimpse through

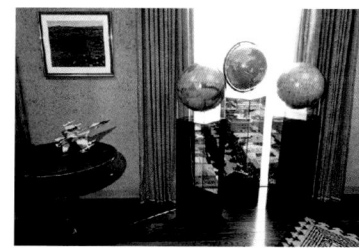

Northrop Corporation

a window to the outside world. For example, a photograph made inside the Northrop Corporation (an aerospace firm with large military contracts) depicts three globes (Mars, Earth, and the moon) atop smoked-glass pedestals. A model fighter jet in camouflage paint seems ready to launch at them. Behind

[5] Britt Salvesen, "Speaking to the Present: The Early Photographs of Lynne Cohen," *Occupied Space* (New York: Aperture, 2012).

[6] Britt Salvesen, "New Topographics," *New Topographics* (Gottingen: Steidl, 2009), 21.

the globes the piercing sun blazes, but the smoked glass acts like a neutral density filter, enabling one to look through and down to a tree-lined street of modest apartment buildings, an incongruous setting for a defense contractor.

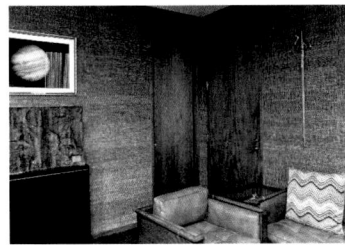

Jupiter and Sabre

More typical of Ressler's photographs is *Jupiter and Sabre*. As in much of Ressler's work, the camera is pointed at the corner of a room, in this case an office lobby. Two doors may lead into inner offices, but the doors are closed, shutting us (and any possible occupants) out. Thus, viewers must attend to the details of the room itself: an uncomfortable-looking chair with stiff wooden arms and low back, the textured-fabric wall covering and a framed photograph of Jupiter that reflects a curtained window. That photograph and a sabre hanging on the opposite wall are meant to signify something to those who wait in this room. Precisely what they are meant to signify, however, is unclear. Is it power? Is it exoticism? Is it a reference to earlier, colonial times? It's an ambiguous space, a holding pen for those seeking access to the more important (and exclusive) interior spaces.

There is ambiguity in many of Ressler's photographs that include people, too. In *White Blazer* we are clearly in an inner office, but of what sort? A man stands confidently behind his desk in a double-breasted white suit jacket; he's young and bearded, his hair coiffed in an unmistakably 1970s fashion. Two empty chairs are on the other side of the

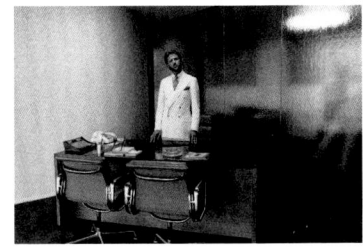

White Blazer

desk, their backs to us. He has a small stack of magazines, a pen holder, a telephone, and an intercom system. Behind him is a wall of wavy, semi-transparent glass through which we can see what looks to be a person leaning over another who is leaning back in a chair of some sort. Is it a dentist's office? Is it a mannequin instead of another person back there? It's unclear, but the eerie disembodied legs seen through the frosted glass echo the executive's unseen legs behind the desk.

Some of Ressler's photographs are almost soul-crushing in what they say about corporate culture. Take for example *Cloud Break*. What a sad, sad room this is. It's either a cafeteria or a break room and there is some small effort made to provide workers with a respite from the cold business interior. Painted on the

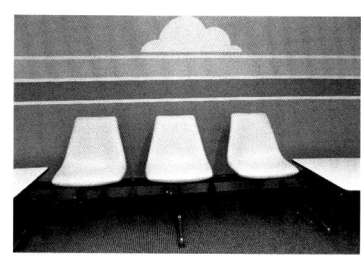

Cloud Break

wall is half a fluffy cloud, its bottom cut off by some horizontal stripes one has to imagine go all the way around the room. An arrangement of modular seating lines the wall—three armless chairs whose fiberglass or plastic bodies you can almost feel flexing rigidly against the small of your back, and two low end tables devoid of any signs of life. They rest on a ribbed rug specially made for high traffic areas. Whatever business is being conducted in the building, the company seems to be adhering to the letter of whatever law that mandates a break room must be provided for workers. But in this case, they've gone out of their way to make sure that there is nothing in this room to entice workers to linger. Take your fifteen-minute break and then head back to your desk; better to be working than to spend time loafing in here!

So what has become of these markers of the new 1970s economy that Ressler preserved so meticulously in *Executive Order*? How have they fared over the past forty years? Columbia Savings and Loan was at the center of the savings and loan crisis of the 1980s that was brought about as a direct effect of Ronald Reagan's deregulation of the thrift industry. In fact, Columbia bought more junk bonds than any other savings institution in the 1980s. It was taken over by the federal government in 1991. Its quick rise and even faster fall serves as a metaphor for much of the American economy under unbridled capitalism. Ressler's photograph alludes to that threat, with a microfiche reader blocking access to an iconic Statue of Liberty printed on an office wall tapestry.

Another financial institution photographed by Ressler had a very different fate, though it no longer exists either. Kyowa Bank, its Los Angeles office having opened in 1978, merged with Saitama Bank, also a Japanese firm, in 1991. At the time of the merger, their combined holdings of $177 billion created one of the world's largest banking conglomerates. They were renamed Asahi Bank, which, in keeping with established patterns of mergers and spinoffs, became something else yet again. Ressler's photograph *Kyowa Bank* accentuates a pattern of diamonds, from the design of the rug to the glass table to the stark ashtray centered on it (ashtrays

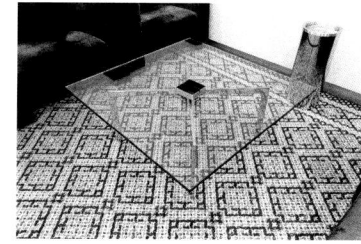

Kyowa Bank

abound in these corporate suites!). The hard angles and edges that dominate the photograph are only partially offset by the plush velvet upholstery on the surrounding chairs.

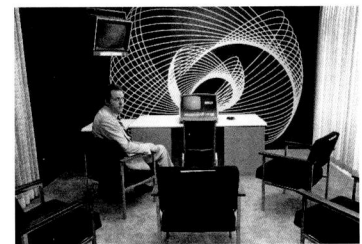

System Development Corporation

System Development Corporation (SDC), a Santa Monica firm that Ressler photographed, went through a merger similar to that of Kyowa Bank. It was sold in 1980 to the Burroughs Corporation, which, in turn, merged with the Sperry Corporation in 1986 to form Unisys Defense Systems. To the extent that anything remains of the original company, it can be found in something called L-3 Technologies. In Ressler's photograph, an anxious worker sits by a small computer console, chairs arrayed around it as though anticipating a dramatic demonstration of its computing powers. On the far wall, a design that seems drawn by a giant Spirograph is meant to convey a future of possibilities. From the vantage point of 2017, however, it comes across as hopelessly dated, dramatic evidence that the future is almost never what those in the past thought it would be.

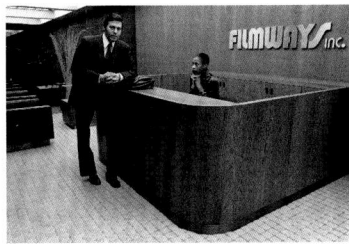

Filmways

Filmways, too, has disappeared. In 1982 it was acquired by Orion Pictures, which went bankrupt nine years later, and then struggled through the rest of the 1990s before disappearing in 1999. In Ressler's photograph, made at the apex of this corporation's success, a white male executive leans nonchalantly against a reception "box" where an African American woman is compliantly on display. While the "boss" looks at us, she looks up at him, her chin resting on her hands. Her look is decidedly not one of demurral or subservience, however. Indeed, she seems completely unimpressed by him. He can't see her looking at him this way, but we have the privilege both to hold his gaze forever and to see how at least one of his employees really feels about him.

Many of the other companies Ressler photographed have also seen their lights dim, though their names linger on. Northrop merged with Grumman in 1984. The Northrop Grumman Corporation is now a leading defense and security contractor with revenues of $24 billion in 2016. In 2002 the company purchased TRW (another company photographed by Ressler), a former Fortune 500 powerhouse that still had more than 120,000 employees in 2000. Somehow, despite all of the merging and gobbling that occurred over the years, Northrop Grumman today has only about half that number of employees. While Vidal Sassoon remains a well-known hair care company, the man himself sold off all of his business interests in the early 1980s. A&M Records ceased operations in 1999 when it merged with Geffen Records and Interscope Records. In 2007, the name was revived and lasted for six more years, disappearing again in 2013.

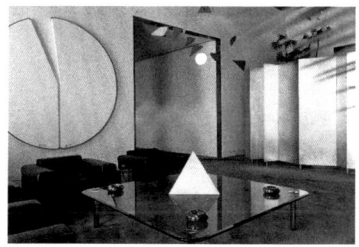

Atlantic Richfield Company (ARCO)

And how about Atlantic Richfield Company (ARCO), where a white-gloved black employee moved a golden pyramid to "center stage" on a glass table so that Ressler could compose what might be her most geometrically complex photograph. When Ressler made that image, the company was nearing its peak, though nobody really knew it yet. A perpetual top-twenty fixture on the Fortune 500 list of businesses, ARCO peaked at number 10 in 1982 before beginning its slide. In 1977, it merged with the Anaconda Copper Mining Company of Montana. Soon thereafter, the price of copper plummeted and ARCO suspended its mining operations. In 1985, the Atlantic brand was spun off on the East Coast, and by 1988 it had been acquired by Sunoco. In 2000, BP America purchased ARCO and then sold it to Tesoro in 2012. In 1982, Atlantic Richfield was listed tenth on the Fortune 500 list. In 2017, Tesoro was ranked ninety-eighth. So, the ARCO name lives on, but mostly as a shiny sign posted outside of the ampm minimart chain. How the mighty have fallen.

———————————

If a young photographer today were to take on the same subject as *Executive Order*, how different would their photographs look? What would be the same? How would they be able to get access without the clout and approbation of the NEA? And what methods and photographic practices would they use? We know that the ashtrays that populate most of Ressler's photographs would all be gone. The style of furniture would be different today, with more emphasis on ergonomic design (Aeron chairs, standing desks) for worker comfort. However, it would be a mistake to see improvements in workplace design as symbols of a more humanistic corporate culture. That hasn't changed much in the last thirty or forty years. New photographs by collaborative artists Paolo Woods and Gabriele Galimberti make that visible in their book, *The Heavens* (Dewi Lewis, 2015), an exposé of corporate excess on a global scale. And Ressler, too, is continuing her project, but in digital color outdoors, shooting consumers in shopping districts around the world.

Corporations clearly continue to exist to maximize profits, and there is ample evidence that any benefits that accrue to workers are only incidental to that larger aim. So better lighting and better ventilation, lactation rooms and employee gyms, healthy snacks and Fiji Water are there to improve the bottom line, whether that be in terms of worker productivity or in terms of worker retention. In other words, while the surfaces may be different, the core of corporate America remains largely unchanged. Profits still preempt people.

Perhaps that will change at some point in the future. The current global wave of populist anger at the status quo suggests that we are ripe for some kind of widespread economic transformation. So too does the rapid increase in automation and artificial intelligence that will displace more and more workers from the jobs that exist now. What that means for the American economy and for American society over the next thirty to forty years is impossible to predict. As the photos in this volume remind us, no one can know what the future will bring. That's what makes *Executive Order* so compelling: It shows us what some of the power elites in the 1970s once thought with great confidence or arrogance their future would be. Learning from the past (and Ressler's photographs) might therefore be one way to create a more humane and sustainable future.

BIOGRAPHIES

Susan Ressler is a renowned artist, author, and educator who has been making social documentary photographs for more than forty years. Her work is in the Smithsonian American Art Museum, the Library and Archives Canada, and many other important collections. A recipient of two National Endowment for the Arts (NEA) fellowships, Ressler is widely exhibited and her photographs have been published in numerous catalogs as well as the journals *Exposure*, *Ten.8*, and *Camera*.

Ressler edited and partially authored the book *Women Artists of the American West* (McFarland, 2003), a scholarly anthology that featured under-represented women artists west of the Mississippi River in fifteen groundbreaking essays by notable authors including Martha A. Sandweiss, Peter E. Palmquist, and Tee A. Corinne. In tandem with this book, Ressler developed one of the first online courses and web archives about women artists at Purdue University, where she was Head of the Photography Area and taught photographic practice, theory, and history in the Department of Visual and Performing Arts from 1981 to 2004. She is currently Professor Emerita, Purdue University, and continues to make photographs that critique consumer culture and other socially relevant issues that shape the world as we know it today. She makes her home in Taos, New Mexico.

Mark Rice is an award-winning author and the founding chair of the American Studies Department at St. John Fisher College near Rochester, New York. He has published two books and contributed essays on photography and visual culture to scholarly journals such as *History of Photography*, *American Quarterly*, *Exposure*, and *Reviews in American History*.

Rice's first book, *Through the Lens of the City: NEA Photography Surveys of the 1970s* (University Press of Mississippi, 2005), examined an important but previously overlooked endeavor to photograph American cities during the bicentennial era. Administered by the National Endowment for the Arts from 1976 to 1981, these surveys included the Los Angeles Documentary Project, possibly the most significant record of the Los Angeles area from that time period. Rice's second book, *Dean Worcester's Fantasy Islands: Photography, Film, and the Colonial Philippines* (University of Michigan Press, 2014, and Ateneo de Manila University Press, 2015) discussed efforts to use photography to promote an American imperial agenda in the Philippines in the early years of the twentieth century. It won the Gintong Aklat (Golden Book) Award for the social sciences, one of the most prestigious publishing prizes in the Philippines, and was also a finalist for the Philippine National Book Award in History.